PRAISE FOR
THE MASK OF MASCULINITY

"This is one of the most important topics today that seemingly no one is talking about: how men can take care of their emotional health in a twenty-first century that demands it. Crucial reading for any young or struggling man."

—**MARK MANSON,** #1 *New York Times* bestselling author of
The Subtle Art of Not Giving a F*ck

"The rigid ideas our culture teaches us about masculinity and femininity make it nearly impossible for real men and women to truly see and love each other. For men who want to free themselves from cultural cages—Howes' book is a life changer. For women who want to offer the men in their lives permission to be fully human— *The Mask of Masculinity* is a vital tool. This book has the power to change lives, relationships, and our culture."

—**GLENNON DOYLE MELTON,** author of #1 *New York Times* bestseller
Love Warrior and founder of Together Rising

"Lewis's raw truth of what it's like to be raised as a male athlete in today's world is exactly what we need to hear. I want every football player (and athlete) to read this book so they can understand what's possible when they take the helmet off."

—**STEVE WEATHERFORD,** Super Bowl Champion, 10-year NFL veteran,
Fittest Man in the NFL, father of five

"For women, reading this book will help them to understand the men in their lives on a much deeper level—and show them ways that they can support the men they love."

—**GRETCHEN RUBIN,** #1 *New York Times* bestselling author of
The Four Tendencies and *The Happiness Project*

"In his new book, *The Mask of Masculinity*, Lewis Howes gives us permission to honor our vulnerability so we can create deeper connections and live a better life. There's nothing sexier than our authentic truth and this book helps us harness it! Lewis transcends gender in this book—it's just as much for women as it is for men."

—**GABBY BERNSTEIN,** #1 *New York Times* bestselling author of
The Universe Has Your Back

"Lewis Howes is going to help a lot of men with this book."

—**DR. DREW PINSKY,** board-certified internist, addiction
medicine specialist, and media personality

"Lewis blends vulnerability, insight, and profound courage to a conversation so deeply needed in this pivotal time of dismantling of a stifling and violent patriarchy. May his integrated voice echo loudly and widely as an invitation to provide more freedom and love within masculinity."

—**ALANIS MORISSETTE,** Grammy award-winning singer-songwriter,
musician, record producer, and activist

"The single most important book I've read on what it means to be a man. I laughed. I cried. It's a page turner that will rock you. If you're raising a son, read this book. Have a father or a brother? Read this book. Just read this book. You'll love it and be a better human because of it."

—**MEL ROBBINS,** award-winning CNN commentator, bestselling author
of *The 5 Second Rule*, entrepreneur, and mother of three

LEWIS HOWES

THE MASK OF MASCULINITY

HOW MEN CAN EMBRACE VULNERABILITY, CREATE STRONG RELATIONSHIPS, AND LIVE THEIR FULLEST LIVES

RODALE.

This is dedicated to every human who has felt heartache, uncertainty, or confusion in relationships with others or, most importantly, with yourself. You are not alone, and we are all in this together.

Copyright © 2017 by Lewis Howes

All rights reserved. Published in the United States by Rodale Books, an imprint of Random House, a division of Penguin Random House LLC, New York.

rodalebooks.com

Rodale Books is a registered trademark, and the plant colophon is a trademark of Penguin Random House LLC.

Originally published in hardcover in the United States by Rodale, an imprint of the Crown Publishing Group, a division of Penguin Random House LLC, New York, in 2017.

Library of Congress Cataloging-in-Publication Data is available upon request.

ISBN 978-0-593-13532-7
Ebook ISBN 978-1-623-36863-0

Printed in the United States of America

Book and cover design by Amy King
Cover photographs by Jared Polin/FroKnowsPhoto.com (main);
other photos by Nick Onken, Dan Robinson, Joshua David Curtis, Spencer Combs, Blamek Eiermann, Chris Guillebeau, Tiff Tyler, and Michael Wahba

10 9 8 7 6 5 4 3 2 1

First Paperback Edition

CONTENTS

Preface vii

INTRODUCTION 1

THE STOIC MASK 17

THE ATHLETE MASK 41

THE MATERIAL MASK 61

THE SEXUAL MASK 83

THE AGGRESSIVE MASK 109

THE JOKER MASK 131

THE INVINCIBLE MASK 153

THE KNOW-IT-ALL MASK 175

THE ALPHA MASK 195

Conclusion 213

Acknowledgments 224

Endnotes 226

Index 233

PREFACE

mask \mask\ *noun*. 1: a cover or partial
cover for the face used for disguise. 2:
something that serves to conceal or
disguise: pretense, cloak

masculinity \mas-kyə-li-nə-tē \ *noun*. 1a:
male. 1b: having qualities appropriate
to or usually associated with a man

—MERRIAM-WEBSTER'S DICTIONARY

HERE IT WAS, the moment I had driven myself toward for more than 5 years. I'd written and sold my first book, *The School of Greatness,* and by leveraging every relationship and calling in every favor I'd ever accumulated, the launch of the book had been enormously successful. Copies were flying off the shelves. It was written about everywhere, from *Forbes* to the *New York Observer.* Midway through the second week after launching, I'd gotten the email from my agent that every author dreams of. "Lewis," he said, "you're debuting at #3 on the *New York Times* bestseller list."

Me. The kid who had trouble reading in school. The one who other kids (and my teachers) thought was dumb. The one whose brother went to prison for selling drugs, who people said I'd grow up to be just like. Not only was I a published author, I was a *New York Times bestselling published author.* And a named bestseller on the *Wall Street Journal, USA Today, Washington Post,* and every other bestseller list you could think of.

I'd never felt higher. My biggest professional dream had come true.

While riding high on my book tour to packed events around the country, I got up and told the story of *The School of Greatness,* passing along the lessons I'd learned from studying under and interviewing some of the most successful athletes, actors, thought leaders, and elite performers in the world. Now with this new achievement, I had a little taste of that greatness myself. Like I said, it's the kind of stuff that dreams are made of.

Yet something nagged at me. Inevitably, at these events, during the Q&A session or afterward at the book signing table, someone would ask me a question that temporarily punctured this bubble of happiness. They'd ask me, "What's next?" or "It seems like you have it all; is there anything missing in your life?" Something about that second question would always catch me off guard. What I had accomplished for myself over the last decade had taken a lot of sacrifice. I was proud of that work, and yet when I looked into the eyes of the person asking me the question, it felt like they saw right through me.

Having just ended a long-term relationship, I spent

each night on the book tour alone, wondering the same thing. The high I had felt on stage or at the signing table in front of a long line of fans and readers deflated. I would feel deep and profound loneliness in an impersonal, nondescript hotel room. I had achieved so much of what I wanted with my book and with my career, but deep down, I was asking myself about the point of it all. I had no one to share it with. I had no intimacy or deep connection with anyone else.

I should have felt amazing, but all I felt was terrible.

One night, after repeating this routine several cities in a row—giving a cheerful answer about my struggle with relationships that, while honest, underplayed the true loneliness I felt—it struck me that this was not a new experience for me. There was another moment in my life where I had achieved my personal goals and reached the pinnacle of success, yet felt utterly unfulfilled with the rewards and alone with my accomplishments: in college, literally as I mounted the podium to accept the honors of becoming a newly minted All-American athlete in the decathlon. Precisely when I should have felt the most overwhelming feelings of pride and confidence and satisfaction, I found myself overcome with depression and doubt.

You might be familiar with this story; I told it at length in *The School of Greatness*. Only I left out a part. The part where, as a young 21-year-old at a very confusing moment in my life, I did what most young men do with confusing feelings: I ignored them. I stuffed them down and pretended they didn't exist. I put them in a box because that's what you are supposed to do if you're a man. Feeling this stuff was just a part of life, and I was weak if I dwelled on it too much. All I knew was that I had to get my life together financially and professionally—the idea that any other concerns mattered was inconceivable to me. Besides, I thought, doesn't becoming successful solve all your problems?

This was rooted in something I learned as an athlete. If something was bothering you, you absolutely 100 percent did not bring it with you on the field. If you were struggling with something in school, that was your problem, and you had better fix it yourself (cheat and lie) or get really good at faking your way through it. Just don't let it impact your performance. As an entrepreneur and media personality, I felt a similar pressure: Show everyone how great your life is going, how much of a badass dude you are, because no one wants to hear your complaints on social media. Toughing it out and then winning, I learned over and over again, was the cure for all that ails. *Especially if you're a man.*

Though I picked up that way of thinking from multiple influences over the course of my life—family, coaches, teammates, movies, media—I knew deep down that there was something wrong with it. In fact, whenever I met truly great performers—athletes like Rich Roll, Ray Lewis, Travis Pastrana, and Steve Weatherford, or motivational speakers like Tony Robbins and Chris Lee—I found that they *didn't* think that way. They weren't stuffing their feelings back down inside themselves. They explored them. They questioned them, and most important, they were aware of them. By dealing with and processing their feelings, they didn't just lift an emotional burden from their shoulders, they found a kind of emotional strength and fuel. The ways these great performers process their emotions have been, and continue to be, awe-inspiring.

There was only one problem: I had no idea how to do

what these men could do. Don't get me wrong, I'd started doing the work on identifying and understanding these feelings. I took seminars and read books. I did one-on-one work with coaches who specialized in working with guys like me. I felt that I knew *what* to do, I just had no idea *how* to do it. So I suffered. I compensated for my insecurities by doing and achieving more, more, more. And it worked, right up until I found myself back in the same position as I had been on the medal stand. Outwardly successful, inwardly unfulfilled and confused.

As the book tour came to a close, I decided the time had come to do things differently. A younger me would have gotten frustrated and given up, or would have heeded the pressure from my school friends to "stop being such a bitch, Lewis" or to "man up and get over it." I didn't want to do that. I couldn't just ignore the anxiety and the uncertainty I felt. I wanted to go beyond exploration and understanding and really figure out how to fix this stuff, so that I could grow and become a better man.

So I could use whatever was bothering me as fuel to grow.

| THE UNIVERSE ALIGNS |

When the book tour ended, I returned home to Los Angeles and realized that the best way for me to grow, and help other men like me grow too, was to dive in deeper and write a book about this very topic, about masculinity and the challenges I face as a man in all areas of my life. Admitting that you are struggling and suffering is important. Recognizing what you are struggling with is just as critical. But understanding *why* you are struggling and *how* to overcome it, well, that's where the magic is. So that's what I set out to do.

At the same time, I started to hear about this documentary by Jennifer Siebel Newsom, called *The Mask You Live In*. Everyone was telling me I had to see it. I thanked the first person who told me about it and put it on my to-do list. I thanked the second person too. By the third, I was intrigued. By the fifth, I said enough already and watched it.

Have you ever watched a movie or read a book that hits you like a ton of bricks? Something that just shakes everything you think you know about the world? Something that feels like it was made especially for you? This documentary was that for me.

The Mask You Live In is about the pressure our masculine culture puts on men and boys to be someone they're not, to ignore their emotions, or worse, to actively fight against them. The movie also talks about the effects this pressure has on male relationships (both platonic and romantic) and on society as a whole. A lot of time in the documentary focuses on inner-city schools, where the profound effects of these issues can clearly be seen. But the issues it deals with are universal to men everywhere.

The Mask You Live In struck me deeply for two reasons. One was serendipity. I'd already decided that my next book would be about masculinity and sold the book to my publisher with the title *The Mask of Masculinity*. It was like the filmmakers could see inside my head. More like they could see inside my heart.

Additionally, the movie affected me deeply because it put crystal-clear language to emotions I was still struggling to get my head around. The documentary opens with Joe Ehrmann, a former NFL football player (one of my first big dreams), talking about what he considers to be the most destructive phrase in our society—*be a man.* It's a phrase every football player has heard from a young age, probably as often as a whistle blow. Certainly, they are three words that have nagged me in the back of my mind for a long time.

The reason I felt so alone after those book signings and the reason it touched such a nerve when people would ask me "How do you do it?" was because I *wasn't* doing it. I'd been with my girlfriend for more than a year during the researching and writing of *The School of Greatness,* only to have the relationship fall apart shortly before the release. As I was out there meeting thousands of people across the country, she was dating other people. My father, due to failing health and serious memory issues from a severe car accident 10 years prior, was not able to even conceptualize what I did for a living. I also discovered that several important friendships had recently ended, right under my nose. Thus, as I was experiencing all this life-changing success, I felt like I had no one to experience it with and no one with whom to share those fears and sorrows. I had just published a book with multiple chapters about the importance of relationships, yet I didn't have the relationships I needed. I was on top of the world in some ways, yet I felt creeping sadness that I couldn't shed. All I had was this voice in the back of my head telling me that there was something wrong with me for feeling this way.

Though I was aware and emotionally capable of processing my feelings, I was in so much pain and in so much conflict with myself that I couldn't use any of these skills. I just felt sad and alone, stuck and uncertain, with no idea why and no idea what to do. What were my options? Pop a pill? Meditate? Lift heavy? Run from the problem? Those are legitimate therapies that work for some people, some of the time, for some of their problems. But I needed something else. I needed to build my vocabulary around my issues so I could speak to them and about them.

This documentary was the first step in teaching me the language of masculinity. It explained for me why men—especially successful men—feel so trapped. As children, we have been put in a box and told to ignore the walls that start to feel like they're closing in around us.

| THE NEXT JOURNEY |

In *The School of Greatness,* I never pretended that I held the secret recipe for greatness. In fact, I never claimed that *I was great.* In that book, I admitted that I was a student yearning to achieve greatness just like everyone else. Thousands of other people could have written some version of this book, but it ended up being me, because I possessed one little advantage: my podcast. In 2013, I started a podcast interviewing high performers and interesting people of all types. This project quickly grew from a hobby into an Internet sensation—to date it's been downloaded more than 35 million times. I am privileged to be able to reach out and interview true greats, from #1 *New York Times* bestselling authors, world-class doctors, and Olympic gold medalists to celebrity influencers, media moguls, and entrepreneurs like Tony Robbins, Larry King, Taye Diggs, Russell Simmons, Arianna Huffington, Gary Vaynerchuk, Ray Lewis, Gabby Reece, Rob Dyrdek, Daymond John, Alanis Morissette, Maria Sharapova, and Mike Rowe. When I wanted to learn about greatness, all I had to do was call up Tim Ferriss or Shawn Johnson or Eric Greitens, ask questions, and let them give me (and my listeners) hours and hours of unmatchable answers.

Amidst my personal crisis of masculinity and happiness, I took solace in knowing that if there was an answer to my questions or a way out of how I felt, then the smart people I got to speak to on my show each week would know it. Somewhat selfishly, I found that in each of my episodes I was asking my guests personal questions that I thought might be of use to me: What's your definition of masculinity? Has it changed from when you were a child to now as an adult? What does it mean to be a man? What's missing in your life? Do you ever feel sad? Do you have any defense mechanisms? What masks do you think you wear?

Off mic and off camera, I would ask even more questions. Whether the responders were men or women, gay or straight, transgender, married or single, their answers were helpful. In fact, the female guests often provided the most honest and the most helpful answers, because they could describe from their own experiences the impact that wearing a mask has *on other people*.

I remember talking to my dear friend Glennon Doyle, who is the super popular blogger and *New York Times* bestselling author of *Love Warrior,* about the disintegration of her marriage and how she and her husband rebuilt it from scratch. She told me that "what it takes for a real man and a real woman to love each other is an incredible unlearning." She said it requires taking apart what our culture has taught us about what it means to be a man and what it means to be a woman. To realize how much we've been poisoned. To strip down to who we actually are. To be naked and unashamed in front of each other. That's the kind of relationship I started to realize was possible if I learned how to take off my own mask. I wouldn't have to apologize or hide my masculinity, but I also wouldn't have to use it as a facade.

Of course, I also learned a lot in these conversations about the masks that women struggle with and the pressures and the unfair standards society forces on them (the same goes for the gay men I spoke to, as well as people of different races and different identities). But recounting these observations are for different books by writers much wiser than me.

Hearing about the universality of the male experience and struggle helped me clarify what my next journey would be—not only as a human being but also as an author. I recognized that in my quest to remove the masks of masculinity that I wore, and that were holding me back, I could help other men—and the women in their lives—remove their own. Just as we became *great* together in *The School of Greatness,* together we could become loving, vulnerable, and, most important, *real* men. Together, we could improve the world.

INTRODUCTION

ON THE FIELD, in my personal life, and in my career, I've always subscribed to traditional notions of masculinity. Work hard, be tough, win at all costs, be aggressive, don't be emotional—you know the clichés. I'm a boy from Ohio. It's a factory, farming, football, meat and potatoes kind of place. The way I was taught to deal with my problems was to smash into things as hard as I could—on the football field, maybe in the parking lot too, if necessary.

In this way, I'm like most guys—whether they live in America or Zimbabwe. I was living the way I was taught by my dad, just like his dad taught him, just like we've all seen on television and in the movies. I was following their lead, on the path to becoming a real man. And just like most guys, it worked okay, until it didn't. Sadness slipped in where success used to live. Loneliness and addiction took over for love. And depression blanketed all of it.

I think it's time we ask: Is this lifestyle really working for the men in our society? Consider that, statistically speaking, males underperform in school compared to their female counterparts,[1] have underdeveloped social skills and friendships,[2] and are more prone to bouts of anger and unprovoked aggression brought on by depression.[3] They also are more likely than women to use almost all types of illicit drugs,[4] engage in more reckless sexual behavior, and be an absentee parent when that sexual recklessness results in pregnancy.

These are just a half dozen examples of problems men face that researchers, educators, and psychologists have connected in one way or another to our misguided notions of masculinity. As you might imagine, these problems don't stop with the men they afflict. They ripple throughout society as a whole. In fact, their effect on the male quality of life often results in early death, either theirs or others.

Consider these numbers:

According to the FBI's 2015 annual report on crime in the United States, nearly 88 percent of all homicides are committed by men.[5] Men in the United States are six times more likely to commit suicide than women.[6] Meanwhile, they are significantly *less likely* to seek help from a suicide prevention institution and half as likely simply to visit a doctor.[7] And this trend starts early in the lives of men. One of the psychologists featured in *The Mask You Live In,* Dr. Niobe Way, found that it is when "we began to hear the language, the emotional language, disappear from boys' narratives, that boys begin to have five times the rate of suicide as girls."[8] A suicide prevention study conducted in Switzerland summarized these findings in as blunt and bleak a fashion as possible: "Women seek help—men die."[9]

Over the years, many well-meaning men and women have tried to address these problems from a variety of angles. Some thought the solution was to teach men how to "get in touch with their feminine side" or "get in touch with their emotions." Others have invented ridiculously divisive terms like "metrosexual" and "alpha male." Men have been lectured and harangued and criticized for being too much of this and not enough of that. These so-called experts promise us better relationships, more personal happiness, and solutions to all our personal problems.

Like many guys, I've had certain books recommended to me—or rather, had a girlfriend or a relative try to push them on me—and yet, I never found any that resonated. Not because I have everything figured out or I'm perfectly well-adjusted, but because more often than not, the advice was condescending and impractical or just plain wrong. I couldn't relate to the people trying to tell me these things.

It was a real shame.

Which is why, in this book, I want to do something completely different.

I'm not going to lecture anyone. I'm not going to criticize. More than that, *I'm not going to try to change you*. I don't think men are fundamentally flawed or broken. Not at all. They are just trapped. I know that's the way I felt for 30 years of my life. Remember those boxes we stuffed our emotions into when we were younger? As we outgrew the boxes, they transformed into masks that hold us back and hurt our friends, family, career partners, and intimate lovers.

The simple purpose of this book is to show you what those masks are, why they're there, and how to take them off. I don't want to change you. I just want to help you be who you already truly are. If you're a woman, I want you to be aware of why men wear certain masks, how you can communicate with men when they are hiding behind them, and how you can support and inspire men to slowly remove these masks.

Am I saying that most men are not being true to themselves? Yes.

Let's look at the traditional depiction of a "real man." A real man must *always* be:

- ▶ Successful at everything he does
- ▶ Physically fit
- ▶ Strong
- ▶ Skilled at fixing things
- ▶ Good at sports or, at the very least, knowledgeable about them
- ▶ Attractive enough to women to be able to get in bed with them

At the same time, a real man must *never* be:

- ▶ Interested in what women think about his appearance
- ▶ Too emotional
- ▶ Afraid
- ▶ Without the answer to a problem
- ▶ Anything but first, most, or best
- ▶ Seen crying—not ever

If you think those are dated clichés I gathered together to make my point, let me point you to an experiment that English teacher Celine Kagan conducted over the course of 4 years from 2008–2012 at Little Red School House and Elisabeth Irwin High School in Manhattan with high school juniors and seniors in a class she specifically designed to "deconstruct the myth of masculinity." She gave her students 10 minutes to respond to a simple prompt:

"What is a man?" Their answers matched almost word for word the phrases I just listed off for you.

As Kagan describes so beautifully, here's how the process unfolded and how ridiculously skewed it tended to be:

> *Inevitably, the discussion that follows begins with a student positing, "A man is someone with a penis." From this point, the conversation moves into a listing of male stereotypes: strong, tough, tall, rich, brave, independent, likes cars, doesn't cry, has lots of sex, watches sports and pornography, etc. I write this list on the board, creating a powerful visual for the students to critique. "Does this list represent what the men you know are really like?" I ask them. Their answer is always, "No."* [10]

Each of us will have a slightly different definition of what it means to be a man—a little bit more of one trait, a little bit less of another—but no matter what, the recipe will always add up to the same impossible creation. No human being could ever successfully live up to the standards we've constructed. Few ever even come close.

Yet falling short can have dire consequences: Men who are deficient in any of these categories are called soft, weak, and stupid. Other men in society label them as gay, losers, bitches, girls, or pussies. To disagree publicly with any of these notions of masculinity is to risk being made fun of, beaten up, or lumped in with these categories yourself.

I know. I remember one day in fourth grade at Smith Elementary School in Delaware, Ohio, my teacher decided that instead of going out for recess on our own, we would all play dodgeball together. I'm not sure if he did this intentionally, but he picked two of the popular boys to be team captains for the game. In standard playground fashion, each boy then chose one classmate after another to join their team until everyone had been selected.

I remember standing there, expecting to be picked early as part of a strategy to build a good team. I was one of the better athletes in class, so I wasn't being egotistical, I was just being logical. The captains, being boys, started by picking boys. I was the tallest kid in class, so they couldn't miss me, but boy after boy was chosen before me. Then the last boy besides me, a kid who was notorious for having no athletic abilities at all, was chosen. Being the last boy picked hurts, a lot. But as a 9-year-old, that pain doesn't compare to the humiliation of not being picked at all, of watching as the two captains called out the girls' names one after another until the very last girl—a girl whom I could lap around a track in a sprint—was chosen. I was the only person left. By default I ended up on the team with the tough luck of having to pick second.

Like many kids, I'd been bullied and teased before, made fun of, picked on, and laughed at. But not like this. This was in front of all my classmates. I was made to appear not only less than the other guys, but I was shown to be less even than the girls. It was deliberate and intentional humiliation—for a reason I can't even remember.

In that moment, I decided that I would never be picked last in sports again. In response to their snub, I set out to "prove" those boys wrong and show them how good I actually was. I went out during that game and literally crushed every single one of them. I returned the humiliation they gave me by dominating them, not only in that inconsequential game of dodgeball but in every game I ever played from that point forward, physically reminding them of their mistakes. I dedicated my life after school to becoming the biggest, fastest, strongest athlete I could become. Without a doubt, this was the fuel for my drive to become All-State in multiple high school sports, a two-sport All-American in college, a pro football player, and then after a wrist injury ended my football career, a USA Men's National Handball Team member. Winning and succeeding in sports made me feel the opposite of how I felt as a vulnerable, picked-on kid.

Do you know what the worst part of my story is? That it's not unique. Nearly every man I know has his own version. The specifics may be different—it could have happened in eighth grade instead of fourth. It might have been a teacher who mocked him for being stupid instead of unathletic. It might have been from a well-intentioned father figure or an early girlfriend. It might have been about money or academics or any number of other topics. It could have turned him into a soldier, a ladies' man, or a billionaire instead of an athlete or an entrepreneur. But almost every man has a story in which he learned—through pain, humiliation, or even force—how he does not measure up. When that happens to him, masks become more than a way to hide; they become armor. In this way, all men—each and every one of us, including myself—have worn or currently wear a variety of masks in order to endure the onslaught of expectations from the world and to live up to the definitions of what it means to *be a man*.

CAN YOU RECOGNIZE THE MASK YOU'RE WEARING?

Over the last few years, I've interviewed hundreds of successful men and women in all sorts of fields. As I began to research the topic of masculinity, I asked the guests on my podcast several questions: What does it mean to be a man? How does this hold people back? What is your greatest fear? *Who are you pretending to be?*

What I learned from them is that all of us have or have had our own insecurities. All of us are, or have been, afraid to be vulnerable and real. Though this fear manifests itself in unique ways for each individual, with their help I was able to uncover nine common masks of masculinity that men wear interchangeably. I've worn almost all of them at some point in my life, and most likely, so have you or someone you know and love.

1. **The Stoic Mask:** Because every man must be invulnerable and tough, emotions are carefully managed and suppressed. There can be no crying, no pain, no feeling. A wall is put up between him and the world to protect him, to pretend he doesn't feel the things he does, because weakness is an invitation to scrutiny and judgment and rejection.

2. **The Athlete Mask:** One of the clearest ways a man can distinguish himself is on the field or on the court. He is like a modern-day gladiator whose weapon isn't death, but domination. Sports are how men prove themselves, and a good athlete is a good man—period. This means spending hours in the gym to get in shape. It means fighting through injuries and pain and fear to win at all costs. And of course, if for some reason a man isn't *good*

at sports, he had better compensate for that by loving them and knowing everything he can about them.

3. **The Material Mask:** There is no clearer sign of a man's worth than the amount of money in his bank account. Not only do men work incredibly hard—and sometimes do questionable things—to make as much money as possible, it's all for naught if other people *don't know how much money he has.* In this way, his cars, his watches, his houses, and his social media feeds become a representation of who he is. A man's net worth becomes his self-worth.

4. **The Sexual Mask:** A man is defined by his sexual conquests—his worth is determined not only by his bank account but by the number of women he's slept with. Relationships? Those are for lesser men—for quitters and settlers. A real man loves them and then leaves them—but he's so good in bed, they're left fully satisfied, of course.

5. **The Aggressive Mask:** Men are aggressive. It's their nature. They're violent and tough, and they never back down. When they see something they want, they take it. Men *hate;* men have enemies. Of course they have a temper; of course they break things; and of course they get into fights. They're the hunters, not the gatherers. It's what men do. A man who thinks otherwise is not a man and is responsible for the weakening of the world.

6. **The Joker Mask:** A man has a sense of humor and a wit that can repel even the most withering critique or the most nagging doubt. Talk about his problems? Okay, Dr. Phil, maybe later. Cynicism and sarcasm and a sense of superiority, these are the intellectual weapons that a man uses to defend against every attempt to soften him

or connect with him. If you want a man to let you in, expect a knock-knock joke, not an open door.

7. **The Invincible Mask:** A man does not feel fear. A man takes risks. Whether that's betting his life savings on a company or cliff diving or smoking and drinking in incredible quantities, a man doesn't have time to think about consequences, he's too busy *doing*. Other people (i.e., women and betas) have "problems." But men? Men have it all under control. They've "got this" and they'll be fine.

8. **The Know-It-All Mask:** A man is not only physically dominant but intellectually dominant too. If you don't understand why that is, a man is happy to explain it to you—along with all the other subjects he's an expert in. He went to a top school, he watches the news, and he knows *all* the answers. He certainly doesn't need your— or anyone's—help. He knows it all.

9. **The Alpha Mask:** At the most basic level, men believe that there are only two types of men: alphas and betas, winners and losers. No man can stand to be the latter— so a man must dominate, one up, and win everything. A man can't ever defer. As a man, he must be in control, and he can't ever do anything a beta (or a woman) would do.

| TAKING OFF THE MASK ISN'T EASY |

The writer John Updike once observed that "celebrity is a mask that eats into the face." I think what he meant was that celebrities, forced to perform and be "on" constantly, lose a sense of their real selves. Masculinity is a similar mask. And unlike the perils of fame, this is a problem that affects more than 0.001 percent of the population.

Many of us have worn our masks for so long that we're not even sure what's actually underneath anymore. We've lost track of where we end and the mask begins, of who we really are. That's why removing the mask is not only terrifying, it's painful. They've fused to our faces. This will not be an easy journey—though I will do my best to make the book easy to read. My own journey required confronting serious pain in my life. I had to face and sit with moments I would have much rather forgotten, things that I held on to and wasn't willing to share with anyone for the first 30 years of my life. These weren't just things that were done to me; I had to accept and acknowledge things I had done to other people—men and women alike.

However, it's in the most difficult and challenging moments that we find the most meaning. An easy journey isn't a journey at all—it's just a walk in the park. In my journey of waking up and trying to pull off my masks in the lead-up to writing this book, I went from a passive-aggressive, egotistical, easily triggered, stuck in the stereotype "dumb jock," to an inspired and inspiring, empowered and empowering, approachable and compassionate, loving . . . man. Not only did my business explode, but my relationships became richer with men and women, and my life is more fulfilled because of it.

Do I still catch myself wearing my masks from time to time? Absolutely! I'm still human. Triggering situations can at times set me off, and in those moments I do and say things that aren't who I want to be. But because of the work I've done over the years, I'm now aware of it when it happens and I'm able to make amends. Most importantly for my growth, I'm able to laugh at myself with my masks on and take them off much more quickly so that I can live the loving life I desire.

Stripped of the various masks of masculinity, we're free to be who we actually are. We can love. We can find our purpose. We can connect. We can actually work harder, do more, be better, and appreciate every step of the way. That's what I am proposing we try to do here together.

| WHY WE NEED TO DO THIS WORK |

I am not proposing an exploration of masculinity for political, biological, or even anthropological reasons. While all of these would be valid reasons, they are certainly above my pay grade. Instead, I have written this book to encourage you to remove your masks for one simple reason: It will make you a better and more successful person in all areas of your life.

Regardless of gender, the key to success in life is creating meaningful *relationships*. You cannot reach financial freedom, become an Olympic gold medalist, have a loving family, solve any of the world's problems, or achieve your wildest dreams on your own. Doing anything great requires creating a team and fostering important relationships that develop and support you along your journey.

I have spoken to many successful entrepreneurs, athletes, inventors, designers, and writers. Regardless of their reputation, I have found that what lies beneath was a caring, empathetic, and insightful person. There was no way they could have accomplished what they did without empathy and insight—and certainly their success would not have lasted long if they did not have them. In fact, when we discussed their mistakes and darkest periods, inevitably what came up were regrets about selfishness, ego, aggressiveness, and a refusal to listen to the feedback from the world around them—all of it driven by a fear of vulnerability.

Contrary to what much of our culture tells us, invulnerability was a weakness that threatened their success, not a strength that supported their achievements. The obvious irony is that from a place of vulnerability, many new ways of existing in the world open up: honesty, compassion, acting for the good of others and without ego, and the ability to heal from one's own wounds. As Dr. Brené Brown wrote, there is nothing weak about vulnerability. On the contrary, it "sounds like truth and feels like courage. Truth and courage aren't always comfortable, but they're never weakness."

There are many things that our definition of masculinity inhibits, but the damage it does to our relationships and sense of self, and therefore to our chances of success in life, should be enough to make you reconsider the stereotypical definition of "masculinity." For that reason, I'm going to be making my case for removing the masks of masculinity for the most selfish of reasons: It will make *you* better, make *you* happier, and make *you* more successful. The fact that these choices may ripple through your relationships and the world as a whole in a positive way—that's just a bonus.

| A NOTE ABOUT THIS JOURNEY |

This is going to be a book that sets forth a new definition of what it means to be a "real man." My goal is to support every man and woman as they work to unlock their full potential, achieve their dreams, and live happy, fulfilled lives. But I want to make it clear that I'm not a scientist or a psychologist, and I'm definitely not a doctor. Just as I would never claim that I am "great" and therefore qualified to lecture anyone (I'm a student like you), I hope that you don't think I am writing this book to shame or talk down to anyone. This research and journey is as much for me as it is for you.

Thus, before you start reading the chapters, I want to provide the following disclaimer: If you see me criticize any behavior in this book, you can be certain that I myself have been guilty of that specific behavior—or *worse*—in my own life. We all have things that hold us back from who we were born to be, from our authentic, most powerful selves, and I am no exception. I'm on the same journey as you. On top of that, if you find any wisdom or insight in this book, rest assured that the source is not me. Instead, the likely source is one of my mentors or one of the "greats" I spoke to in the course of this research. It has been my intention from day one to be a conduit for them, and if I bring anything to the table as a writer and thinker, it's in my ability to gather their insights all together in one place and organize their observations into an actionable format.

I also want to say something about gender throughout this book: Many of my examples, stories, and interviews are with men. And I am a man. The book includes masculinity in the title. But for the women reading this, rest assured that there is plenty in here for you. We all struggle with these masks throughout our lives, whatever our gender. Understanding these masks of masculinity can help you decode the men in your life—and shed light on your own biases too.

What I don't want to do—and what I hope I haven't done—is imply that men somehow have it harder or that women have it easier. This is a personal book; that's why I use the word *I* in it. This is a book about a very real set of struggles I've had, and so if you hear the voice of a man fighting his own fights throughout this book, that's exactly how it was meant to be. My hope is that in those struggles you can find something approaching guidance—maybe even solace—regardless of whether you are a man or a woman.

I hope that with the brave insights and experiences of every person mentioned in this book, we can all find something worth learning, something we can apply in our own life, and something to spark meaningful conversations. Using the prescriptions provided at the end of each Mask chapter, I believe it's possible for men to evolve into a new modern-day archetype that can help them lead powerfully in business, express courageously in relationships, find inner peace and happiness along the way, and become a sounding board for women and other men in their lives so that all may understand their roles and lift each other up in this process.

It's time to unmask.

THE
STOIC
MASK

You don't like this role of
bird with broken wing,
especially since that's
exactly how you feel.

—JAY MCINERNEY, *BRIGHT LIGHTS, BIG CITY*

AT SOME POINT, every man has fantasized about being a **hero.** A hero is a fearless badass who always comes through when the world is about to crash. When we are young, many of us dream of becoming a superhero. But as we get older, we come to understand that men with capes don't actually exist. We learn, instead, that the real heroes are the firefighters, the police officers, the soldiers, the first responders, and any men of service out there saving lives. They are men who rush into burning buildings or the line of fire to save someone else; men who put away their dreams of capes and costumes for the reality of uniforms and sacrifice.

For most of us, this life is also a fantasy. Deep down, we're too scared to do any of it. I remember there was a moment in high school when I thought, "Maybe the military is something I would do." But then after some exploration, I realized just how hard that would actually be, so I moved on to the next thing—something I thought would be easier. I went from, "I want to be a Navy SEAL" to "I want to be an All-American and a professional athlete." In each case, the dream was the same: to be a hero. The leader. A man who represents the greatness of his country, a man who doesn't feel pain, and a man who does amazing things. Except now, as an athlete, if I failed at this dream, I wouldn't die.

In the summer of 2016, I was lucky enough to spend some time with Captain Dale Dye of the United States Marine Corps. Dale spent 20-plus years in the Marines. He conducted 31 combat operations in Vietnam, received a Bronze Star for heroic achievement, earned three (!) Purple Hearts, and was wounded five times. Before retiring in 1984, he was part of the peacekeeping forces in Beirut during the Lebanese Civil War. If you are like most people, or like me, you probably knew none of that. You may have never even heard of Captain Dale Dye. But I can almost guarantee that you have seen him in uniform, or watched something military-related for which Dale was responsible.

You see, after Dale Dye left the Marines, he not only acted in movies such as *Platoon* and the HBO miniseries *Band of Brothers*, but in 1985 he created a company that has done more than any history book ever could do to explain, communicate, and document the experience of what it is like to be a soldier. The company, Warriors, Inc., is responsible for training actors like Tom Hanks, Willem Dafoe, Sean Penn, Damien Lewis, Colin Farrell, and Tom Cruise for movies and TV shows such as *Platoon, Casualties of War, Born on the Fourth of July, Saving Private Ryan, Band of Brothers,* and *The Pacific.*

If you've seen a realistic war movie in the last three decades—if you've seen an actor pull off the perfect thousand-yard stare or conquer insurmountable obstacles with perfect courage—Dale and his team are probably responsible. You could argue that for an entire generation of men, our notion of what it's like to be a hero—*to be a man*—is partially due to the amazing work of Dale Dye and the men and women of Warriors, Inc.

Dale is able to do this work because he's a true war hero. He's seen the absolute worst and best of humanity in the jungles of Vietnam and the streets of Lebanon, and he's survived to tell the tale. He sacrificed for his country, for his men, and for his family to do something truly great.

When I sat down with him, Dale was a couple of months shy of his 72nd birthday. Despite his age, he still had that sharp, gravelly drill sergeant's voice that made me sit up and pay attention. It shot out from between a thick white mustache and a square chin that jutted out from his jawline. When I asked him questions, his deep-set eyes looked directly at me from out over a strong nose that had almost definitely taken a punch or two in his day. He's the kind of guy, even as a 71-year-old, you look at and go, "Now that's a tough dude."

The reason I wanted to talk to Dale was to find out what it's like to be a warrior. The two worlds I am most familiar with—sports and business—are filled with so much language around war. In football, quarterbacks are gun-slingers. Games are won or lost in the trenches. In business, it's kill or be killed. But none of that language ever reso-nated with me. I felt kind of phony saying those things. In talking to Dale, I wanted to compare how I felt about being an athlete and an entrepreneur with how he thought about being an actual warrior. I had so many questions: How did he find the strength and resolve to endure what he has endured? How did he conquer his fear? What did it take to re-enter modern society after experiencing something as timeless and primal as war? And most importantly, is there a cost to the warrior life?

When we spoke, he reminded me a lot of the inspiring coaches and father figures I've had in my life. He talked about sacrifice. He talked about struggle. He spoke in a way that made me stiffen up and say to myself, "Forget every-thing, I just want to *impress this guy*" because he is so fear-less, tough, and strong.

Dale also told me a story that I think revealed where he learned the ability to coach. When he was in Echo Com-pany, Second Battalion, Third Marines, Dale had a platoon commander named "Wild Bill" Teehan. Wild Bill was the epitome of the bold, fearless leader. He would lead from the front, and he never showed his men even a hint of weak-ness. There would be bullets flying and men falling down all around them, and Wild Bill would gather himself, look at his soldiers, and say, "Follow me."

The man was so fearless, the men almost thought he was crazy. Does he have a death wish? Is he inhuman? Does he need to be committed? Why isn't he scared? (Where did they think the "wild" in Wild Bill came from?)

One day after a terrible day of fighting near the Cửa Việt River, Dale was taking cover in a foxhole. He was trying to stay awake when Wild Bill made his way over and dropped into the hole. As Bill carried on like everything was fine, and they hadn't just literally fought for their lives, Dale decided he would ask what was on Wild Bill's mind. He figured he might not make it through to the next day, so he might as well ask what this guy's deal was, since he might not get another chance.

Wild Bill Teehan looked at that young soldier and said, "It's just about not letting anybody know how afraid you are. I've got a platoon here that I need to run and I need to inspire and I need to motivate and I need to take care of, and in order to do that, they can't see me afraid, but I am."

Dale thought to himself, "Well, there's a lesson for you."

Like a lot of men, whether they've served or not, Dale internalized a lesson he would remember all his life. You've probably heard and thought it too: "Never let them see you sweat."

Anyone who has ever been in a position of leadership learns that you must maintain a certain bearing. You must project an image of strength or confidence that other people can lean on. If you don't, the people around you feel anxious, scared, or unprotected. No one wants to look up and see their boss cowering when under fire. We want to see them face danger bravely, head-on.

In my previous book, *The School of Greatness,* I told the story of my brother, Christian, who, at 18 years old, was sentenced to prison for selling LSD to an undercover cop. He got out on good behavior after 4 years and has since transformed his life. He is known as one of the greatest jazz violinists in the world, and he teaches thousands of students every year, inspiring them to live a great life as well. I was only 8 years old when he went inside. I remember thinking, even then, at that young, fragile, and impressionable age: "I have to be a man now. I have to be strong for my parents. I can't cry. I can't trouble them with my troubles." Those were my thoughts, as an elementary school kid.

I do think there is something admirable in that mentality, in being strong. Some measure of strength does prevent you from falling apart like a house of cards. The problem is when that toughness doesn't stop and it grows like cancer until it strangles all the other feelings. For me—and for so many other guys—the likelihood of that emotional strangulation is so much greater because we were children when we learned this stuff. We weren't Marines. We weren't trained protectors. We were young. When you're young, you're supposed to be able to lean on other people. Instead, we were taught that even the adults in our lives would be leaning on us. This meant the armor had to go up—and stay up—from the days of our earliest memories.

The night my brother got out of prison, we had a family meeting. Christian sat down and told us how sorry he was for the shame and stress he put on our family and that he felt horrible for letting all of us down. Everyone was crying, even the Japanese exchange student whom we were hosting for 6 months who had never met my brother. Christian was howling-at-the-moon crying, my sisters were clinging to me and bawling their eyes out, my mother and father were an emotional mess, but I didn't tear up at all. With all these people around me being vulnerable and open—including two *male* relatives—there was no reason for me to keep my emotions in, and yet I felt like I didn't have that option. I'd lost that part of myself. And I was only 12 years old.

Even now, as I write this last paragraph, I look at the way I describe my family's emotional response compared to mine. Unconsciously I made theirs seem weak while I made mine feel strong—when obviously the opposite is true. I could edit it, but I'm going to keep it this way, because it's important to recognize that these tendencies are very strong and the work doesn't stop.

As we get older, we carry tendencies like this with us. We don't even remember where we learned them. It could have been a strong word from a relative: "Hey, don't be a wuss." It could have been the teasing of the kids at school. It could have been something we saw on television or in the movies. Likely, it was all of the above.

For men of Dale's generation, it was taken for granted that feelings should never come up. This was especially true of men from Dale's line of work. As he put it to me, "You've got things to do. You've got to face life. Life is not easy. War is not easy. Business is not easy."

It's not just pain from war that men are pretending isn't there. In 2014, the American Medical Association published a study in its peer-reviewed journal *JAMA Psychiatry* revealing that men who have served in the military are twice as likely to report having been sexually abused as a child as compared to their nonmilitary male counterparts. Yet because they can't talk about these things—because it's not manly—they carry the pain around for so long that the trauma often manifests itself in the form of numerous mental health issues, including depression.[1]

No matter how strong they were, men like Dale were

expected to manage, to domesticate their emotions, and to never show them publicly. It occurred to me, though, that military men like Dale had one advantage: They were surrounded by other men who were going through the exact same thing as they were. There is camaraderie in serving shoulder to shoulder with other men and women that doesn't necessarily exist for, say, work-from-home entrepreneurs. In fact, by definition, this generation of workers who sit in front of computer screens all day has less human interaction and is less socially connected than were the men and women of previous generations.

Dale told me that although men and women he served with might not express their emotions openly, when things would build to a breaking point, relationships were always there to catch you. "You go and have a beer," he told me, "and finally you work up the courage to say, 'Hey, this has really screwed me up here.' That's when the friend says, 'Yeah, I get it.' And you talk about it, and there's no expectation between you. That's what a friend really is. They're not demanding of you to feel one way or feel another way. They're your pal, your buddy, and you can just say, 'Look, this has got me up against the rails here. I don't know what I'm doing.' And they're not going to say, 'Well, then you're clearly a weenie.'"

These are wonderful conversations. I've had a few with teammates over the years. These conversations were no more than a few words sometimes, but they were what I needed. Unfortunately, these conversations are not nearly as common or as frequent as they need to be. And the less frequent they are, the worse the negative feedback loop becomes for men who are struggling. These men feel alone with a problem and can't connect about it. Because they can't connect, they struggle to find a solution, and so they feel more alone and the problem gets worse. Often, they'll turn to the women in their life. One study found that 71 percent of married men in the United States selected their wives as the persons they turn to when they are feeling depressed (39 percent of married women turn to their husbands;[2] women have far richer networks of friends, family, and sources of solace when they need help).

In Phil Knight's memoir, *Shoe Dog,* he describes one of the most challenging periods in his business life. He was fighting with his former partners. The United States government had just hit his company, Nike, with a surprise multimillion-dollar tax bill that, if forced to pay in full, would drive him and the company out of business. Worse, the entire issue was one that his competitors had created. They had lobbied behind the scenes, attacking Nike through means other than where it counted: at market, with customers. Knight would come home and try to talk to his wife about all the stress and pain and fear he felt.

"I tried to talk to Penny about it," he writes, "but she said I didn't actually talk, I grunted and stared off. 'Here comes the wall,' she'd say exasperated, and a little frightened. I should have told her, that's what men do when they fight. They put up walls. They pull up the drawbridge. They fill the moat."[3]

I think it's safe to say that nearly every spouse and girlfriend and mother and sister and friend has thought that same thing about a man they cared for at some point in their lives. Knight's wife had been with him since the beginning. She started as one of the first employees of Nike.

She was so dedicated to the company her husband was building that she refused to cash her paychecks in order to help. Yet he was putting up the wall to block even her out. He was *fighting against the person who cared about him most*. Imagine what his kids must have felt. Imagine his parents and his employees too. All of them stuck on the wrong side of the wall, because as the CEO of a young company with numerous enemies arrayed against him, he couldn't afford to show weakness to *anybody*.

Sometimes it's not just the women in your life or your family whom you lock out when you hide behind this mask of strength and unflappability. Sometimes it is the entire world you lock out, and what you are keeping from them is your true, authentic self. The real you.

Robbie Rogers is only the second English-born professional soccer player to come out, and he is an openly gay athlete playing in a major American professional league. His struggle to come out of the closet was profound. Second only to the military, the professional sports world is about as hostile to gays as any you'll ever find. Gay jokes in the locker room aren't just a frequent occurrence; they are often a form of what passes for masculine bonding. Robbie—the *real* Robbie—was by definition on the outside of that, looking in. Naturally, he was terrified of what other people would think about him, including his teammates.

When we sat down to talk about his journey, and I asked him how he managed to finally come out, he shared with me something his mother told him: "Robbie, sometimes you have to give people a chance. Like a chance to just love you and to really know you." Those are wise words, and Robbie is a true hero for listening to them. **Taking off that mask to show vulnerability is one thing, but when you**

do it to show the world who you really are, that is
something else entirely. That is true strength.

Gay or straight, famous or anonymous, many men are afraid to do what Robbie's mom counseled—to love or allow themselves to be loved—because it means making themselves vulnerable to the judgment of other people. Giving people a chance to love and know you leaves you open to the risk that they won't take the chance you're offering. It's much easier to eliminate that risk by retreating behind the mask and showing people only what you think they want to see.

This is one of many costs that traditional masculinity imposes on relationships. With total casualness, Dale mentioned to me that he "went through a couple of marriages." War, starting a business, pursuing a big dream—these are often isolating and consuming tasks. "The whole business of going home to the girlfriend and the hearth and so on and so forth, that's on your mind and that's an added pressure" is the way Dale described it to me. "It is just one of the things you have to deal with." Relationships weren't a source of refuge or strength for him; they were another item on the to-do list.

I've related to that in my life. There is this modern notion that relationships hold us back. "I don't want to be tied down" is what guys say. "I've got so much I still want to do." They feel they need the freedom to pursue their dreams wholeheartedly, and the only way they're going to achieve their goals is to be unfettered by obligations to someone or something else. I've said that. I've broken up with women for that exact reason. But is a relationship really something to "deal with"? Do relationships actually stand in the way of our goals? Unhealthy ones, sure. But good relationships, with open communication, are the exact opposite. They *help us* deal with our dreams and reach our potential. The jury is pretty much in on that notion. In fact, a study published in the *Journal of Personality and Social Psychology* found that encouragement from a partner as you pursue goals in all aspects of your life increases the likelihood that you'll achieve those goals. *And* it will make you happier in the relationship on top of it.[4]

The problem is, being open with our communication and relying in any way on someone else during our journey to success has traditionally been seen as a sign of weakness. Those beliefs are slowly shifting and habits are changing. **Men lag behind this shift because they are still learning how to talk openly with their partners and connect honestly with other men. We know what to do. We just don't know how to do it. And until that changes, where does that leave us? That's right. It leaves us alone.**

A *Chicago Tribune* article based on the work of Terri Orbuch, PhD—a professor at Oakland University and the University of Michigan who has completed long-term studies on marriage and divorce—describes the situation like this:

> *Traditional masculinity distances men from having intimate relationships with other men, and it makes them more dependent on their wives for affection, affirmation, and emotional support. This is, then, why it is harder for men after a divorce or a relationship breakup.*[5]

In a December 2014 post on *Psychology Today,*[6] Elizabeth McClintock, PhD, surveyed a range of studies on this same topic conducted over the previous decade and found that:

> *Not only may marital happiness be higher for men than women, the protective health effect of marriage is larger for men [than women]. In other words, men may be happier in their marriages than women and men may have more to lose in a divorce or breakup in terms of health and happiness.*

This brings us back to Dale. He is happily married now (he remarried at age 61), but not all veterans are so lucky. Studies show that both military men and women have higher rates of divorce than nonmilitary citizens, and that experiencing combat significantly increases the rate at which marriages fall apart.[7] Another study found that 75 percent of married or cohabitating service members and veterans experienced some recent "family problem," whether that was with their spouse or their children. More than 50 percent of veterans who had separated from their partners reported intense or even violent incidents.[8] In other words, the men (and women) who need the benefits of marriage most often have the hardest time getting them.

If all this is true, and I have no doubt that it is, then *what the hell are we doing* (pardon my French) *as men and as a society?!?*

As you've probably figured out by now, at the root of the problem is our toxic understanding of masculinity. Even guys who have been through the ringer and lived to tell the tale—as Dale has—perpetuate it. I asked Dale what kind of advice he would give his 20-year-old self, and the entire exchange is one that continues to rattle me to this day:

> *I'd say this. "Look, you have a role in life. That role has been given to you because you were born with a certain set of genitals and a certain emotional makeup. There's nothing you can do about that. That's a good thing. So play your role. Your role is to be a provider, a defender, a teacher. Your role is to step up in the hard times. Now, that's going to take some doing. It's going to take some thinking. It's going to take some courage. But if you will do it, in the hardest of times, your life will be rewarding no matter how many troubles you go through, no matter how many hard times, no matter how many emotional pits you fall into. If you'll step up and remember that you have this role and that you must perform in that role, your life will be rewarding. Don't let anything pull you off that track."*

I relate to this message. I'm sure a lot of guys do too. But I'm sure a lot of guys *don't* as well. What about those guys? I asked him about those men. "What if that role doesn't resonate with someone? What if there's a young man growing up who's like, 'That doesn't feel right to me.' Or 'I don't feel like that's who I am.'"

I don't know what I thought his answer would be. I know that I didn't expect what he said. I figured as a man who has worked in the creative field of Hollywood for more than two decades, a man who is now happily married and has seen society progress in unimaginable ways, he'd say something that reflected these experiences.

When I asked him what he'd say to a guy who felt some reservations about his so-called "role" as a "provider," Dale paused and then continued, "I would say, 'You're doing way too damn much feeling.'"

No wonder so many men live behind an artificial wall, or hunker down inside an emotional foxhole. No wonder so many men walk around wearing an emotionless, stoic mask. It's because at pivotal times in their lives, they had this very conversation with someone they knew or respected. And in a moment of honesty and vulnerability, someone said to them, "Hey, man, that's way too much feeling."

In an increasingly progressive world, we tend to think that gender stereotypes are so old-fashioned that they're fully in the past. We think that we've moved forward as a society. We obviously haven't. Dale said those words to me in August 2016 as we spoke together. We were not in some bunker in a war zone, but across from each other, wearing casual clothes in my recording studio, in peaceful, sunny Los Angeles. You can dismiss Dale as just another cranky old man. But that's not who Dale is. He is a smart, accomplished man of enormous societal influence who works in an industry that is famously open-minded. And he's not abnormal at all, which is why you have to take him at his word and understand just what that might mean for future generations of young men.

"Raising other people's children" was how Dale described his job in the Corps. Now, he raises *everyone's children*. I imagine him having that conversation with a young Tom Cruise or Matt Damon or Johnny Depp. I don't think it's possible to begin to quantify the impact that Dale Dye has had on our notions of masculinity as a society. He's the guy who trains the badasses that kids see in movies. He's the hero behind the heroes.

Yet, as much as I respect his opinions and beliefs, it's thoughts like the ones he expressed to me that hold so many men and women back from experiencing true fulfillment in life and all that those feelings and emotions have to offer. As a man, he said, you have a role "given to you because you were born with a certain set of genitals and a certain emotional makeup. *There's nothing you can do about that.*"

Nothing? No wonder men feel stuck and depressed and closed off.

I remember lying in bed many years ago, nearly in tears, watching every episode of *Weeds* on Netflix for a span of 2 weeks without leaving my apartment or working out because of the confusion I was facing with my girlfriend. I'd moved to Los Angeles to be with her, which for me at that point in my life was a *huge* leap of faith and a rare demonstration of vulnerability. Yet before I'd even unpacked my bags, she had my emotions on a string and was tying them in knots. She'd change her demeanor from one day to the next: passionate and loving today, negative and passive-aggressive tomorrow. She had me hooked to her connection and intimacy and would use that (by threatening to take it away) to keep me where she wanted me. She was a very emotionally capricious lover. She wanted me, then suddenly, she didn't want me anymore. Back and forth we went. It was exhausting to watch helplessly as she sabotaged our relationship. I couldn't do anything for days on end except lie there numb, because I was so afraid of what my emotional response said about me and my manhood.

I didn't know what to do. I definitely knew I couldn't tell anyone about it. Not my parents, not my friends, certainly not other women. I didn't realize I deserved better, and I didn't have the courage to explore it. So instead I just lay in my bed for 2 weeks straight and watched 80 hours of television. When I finally forced myself out of the apartment and went outside, the mask was firmly in place. Numb, passionless, guarded, unavailable, and definitely lacking the confidence I once had. I was not going to let another woman see me sweat.

I felt like I had no other option.

Or did I?

I spoke with Randy Couture, the six-time UFC world heavyweight and light heavyweight champion, about his definition of manhood. Randy isn't just one of the most decorated mixed martial artists of all time, he's a master of reinventing himself. He began his career as a collegiate wrestler, served as a soldier in the US Army for 6 years, was a four-time US Olympic wrestling team alternate, and enjoyed a hall of fame mixed martial arts career where he became the first of only two UFC fighters to hold two championship titles in two different divisions. And he did all this before becoming a superstar actor for his roles in all three of *The Expendables*, *Ambushed*, and *The Scorpion King 2*, among others. He's recognized as one of the toughest men in the world. I asked Randy about his definition of masculinity, and his perspective was a lot more freeing and accessible than Dale's:

I think just being true to yourself, true to your heart, and being strong enough to let people see that ... I think we have a tendency to put up walls and put up fronts. We're scared to let people in, to let people see really what's going on, really what we feel like, and I think a real man is strong enough and confident enough to open up and let you see.

It was like he'd just gotten off the phone with Robbie Rogers's mom. I asked Randy if a *real man* cries. "I think a real man does," Randy told me. He said a real man expresses his emotions too. "I think you have to, or you're not feeling. You've shut it off so long that you just don't feel anymore, and I think that's not good."

I was glad he expressed it this way, because it matched up with the research I found as I tried to get to the bottom of my own struggle with the Stoic Mask. Fredric Rabinowitz, author of *Deepening Psychotherapy for Men,* found that "once it is reframed as a sign of strength to seek help ... most men find talking and processing their experience therapeutic."[9] When someone as tough and respected as Randy Couture expresses that it's okay for "real men" to be open, to be vulnerable, or even to get help, he's giving us a gift. He's freeing all of us from the prison of the stereotypes and the knee-jerk assumptions that were more common in Dale Dye's generation.

Dr. Brené Brown, author of the bestselling book *Daring Greatly,* points out that this is a step toward real gender equality and fairness. **"Most women pledge allegiance to this idea that women can explore their emotions,** break down, fall apart," she said, "and it's healthy. But guys are not allowed to fall apart."[10]

Randy and Dale recently worked on an independent movie together called *Range 15*. Maybe what we're seeing is a little bit of the passing of the torch. Maybe openness is winning out.

I hope all of this doesn't scare you. No one is saying you have to wake up tomorrow and sing your feelings at the top of your lungs. The journey to remove the Stoic Mask is a long one, and the idea of abruptly tearing it off can be intimidating. But it doesn't have to be.

Chris Lee, author of *Transform Your Life: 10 Principles of Abundance and Prosperity,* has been a leadership and emotional intelligence coach for the past 30 years. During his legendary intimate weeklong workshops, he has trained more than 100,000 men and women. He has some practical advice for men who are looking to slowly dismantle their walls. He says men should start journaling. He tells them to "get out a notebook and just write. You know, 'What are my beliefs about being open? How do I feel or what's my fear about sharing my feelings, my emotions?' And look over those beliefs and ask yourself, which of those beliefs are facts?"

We are driven by our beliefs—the problem is that many of our beliefs aren't beliefs at all. They're faulty assumptions built on fear that get baked into culture because we're even more afraid of addressing them than we are of addressing the fear that created them. We think that being open about our feelings is weak. Straight men have been trained to think that sharing their feelings means they're gay, and if someone ever thought that about them, it would jeopardize their "manhood." We think that if we care about this instead of that, or if we prefer this thing to that thing, there is something wrong with us. We think that, as men of Dale's generation might put it, having a certain kind of genitals means the entire world rests on our shoulders and that there is no room to question any of it.

Are you pretending you don't have feelings? That is not only a lie, it can accomplish the opposite of what you expect. Howard Gardner, a Harvard professor of cognition and education, has written that, **"The less a person understands his own feelings, the more he will fall prey to them. The less a person understands the feelings, the responses, and the behavior of others, the more likely he will interact inappropriately with them and therefore fail to secure his proper place in the world."**[11]

Chris Lee gave me an analogy that has helped a lot. He said our beliefs are like a GPS system, and we listen to them the same way we would Google Maps. **Our beliefs about what it means to be a man—that we must be reserved and tough and solitary—are leading us astray, down a lonely road to nowhere. More specifically, they are holding us back from getting to the place we all know deep down that we want to go.**

I learned that lesson with my own podcast. It has been the site of one of my most important disclosures to date: the fact that, as a young child, I was raped. After years of shame and covering up, I was finally able to open up about the experience. Part of what allowed me to do that was my conversations with Chris and doing the very journaling he recommended. I asked myself, "Why am I so afraid to talk about this?" The answer was that I thought people would judge me, that my trauma somehow said I was less of a man or that there was something wrong with me. The fact that I felt pain about it still, years later, said I was a weakling. After writing down these beliefs, I could clearly see how they were limiting me. Seeing my beliefs on the page in front of me, I recognized that they were just plain factually incorrect.

When I started opening up about it in my writing and to my audience, people would email me and say, "Something you're doing is different. Your podcast was great before, but there's something that's just . . . I can't put my finger on it, but you're just so much more present and connected, and you're a better listener, and you're more caring."

They *noticed*.

When I took off the mask, I was able to share my feelings. I also felt freed up to do better work. This unmasking let my audience see the real me, *and they liked that me better*. The results were great for my business, my relationships, and my health. I feel more confident every day that my audience sees *the real me* and that they appreciate who I am for what I am.

It's not the mask they liked; it's me.

| WHAT CAN WE DO RIGHT NOW? |

My goal is that everything you've just read makes sense to you. If you relate to it, or if what you've read describes the men in your life, then I've accomplished my objective. My intention is to give you a new way of looking at things. But, just to be sure, I want to leave you with something you can start doing right now to begin the process of removing the Stoic Mask and opening yourself up to all the possibilities of the world around you. If the limitations of the Stoic Mask resonate deeply with you, it means that you're basically a heart attack waiting to happen. **What you are suppressing is creating disease. Disease of the heart, the mind, and the soul. You need to clear this by exposing what you're covering up to the light of openness, honesty, and vulnerability.**

What's Available When You Drop This Mask (Stoic)

Remember Stoic Man, you are a gift, and there's so much to celebrate about you. The people who care about you the most have been waiting to see what's behind your mask. It's time to reveal the real you. These are some of the things that can flood back into your life when you drop this mask.

> **Emotional freedom**
> **A weight off your shoulders**
> **Deeper relationships with men and women**
> **Healing**
> **A healthy heart**
> **Vulnerability**
> **The permission to feel**
> **Acceptance and belonging**

MEN:

If you're lost about how to do this, try these few steps first. They aren't a miracle cure; nothing is. But they are important, and they can at least help you get the ball rolling toward dropping this mask. Note: If you feel like any of these steps are dumb, are stupid, or won't work, trust me. I've done them all, and they've worked for me.

1. **Step 1:** Make a list of the five most painful moments of your life. Note what happened, and how you felt in each moment. Journal about it and go into detail. (An example could be: My dad was my best friend growing up, but he abandoned me when I was 6, and it left me devastated.)

2. **Step 2:** Once you've journaled about these painful moments, read them out loud to yourself. Give yourself permission to feel or to cry about them when you hear your own words. Play soft instrumental music during this process to facilitate your ability to reach your emotions as you allow your feelings to awaken.

3. **Step 3:** Share them. When you have accepted the truth of this pain and all these emotions, tell a friend, partner, or family member whom you trust. Part of removing the Stoic Mask is allowing other people to support you. The only way they can do that is if they know what's going on. I'm a big believer that anyone who has experienced trauma in their past (and hasn't ever discussed it with someone) will allow the trauma to grow in negative ways. You won't be able to heal until you begin to share your story.

4. **Step 4:** Look into hiring a coach, therapist, or someone who is a specialist. Once you've shared your pain, you need to find someone who has experience with helping people understand their emotions and get comfortable with them. For those who really struggle behind the Stoic Mask, this is serious work and it requires a serious

approach. But it is work that can start today, right now, with a piece of paper and a pencil.

WOMEN:

Be patient with the men in your life who are struggling with this mask. Listen to them. Ask them to communicate their feelings to you. Be proactive about it. Take the initiative. They most likely won't do it on their own. The gap between verbalizing their emotions to themselves and verbalizing them to a friend or a family member is like walking a tightrope over the Grand Canyon. If you want the man in your life to take off his Stoic Mask, you can lead the way by example and take off your Stoic Mask. Let them know you'll be there to catch them when they start to open up. Just know that underneath his Stoic Mask is a vulnerable man with a big heart who wants to come out and be his real self around you.

THE ATHLETE MASK

[He's a] man who destroys
himself running for a finish
line that doesn't exist.

—WRIGHT THOMPSON

ON JANUARY 30, 1973, the dreams of 23-year-old Joe Ehrmann came true. On that day, he was chosen in the first round of the NFL draft by the Baltimore Colts. He was the tenth overall pick, and he experienced the dream not only of every aspiring athlete, but also the dream of millions of young men around the world—to go *pro.*

We can all vividly remember the team selection process for games at recess during elementary school. Dodgeball, kickball, basketball, soccer. Sometimes we were picked last, and that felt horrible. Other times we were picked in the middle of the pack, and we felt glad just to be on a team. And then every so often we were picked first, and that felt *amazing*.

Imagine that feeling of being picked first for a team, but at an entirely other level. Joe was chosen to play as a professional—he was going to get *paid* for this stuff—in one of the most popular sports in America, by one of the most famous and respected teams in the league. He was over the moon, but he wasn't surprised. Joe had been a good player for a long time. He'd been good in high school. He'd been good in college, playing for Syracuse. He wasn't just good; he was tough too. In 1969, after beating Wisconsin 43–7 in front of 45,000 people, Joe got into a fight with four or five people at the same time, some of whom were fans. One fan stole his helmet as a prize, but he became so afraid about what he'd done that he didn't return the helmet to Joe for 40 years.

Joe was an All-American in 1970 for Syracuse University. He would go on to play eight seasons for the Colts and then two seasons for the Detroit Lions. After the 1976 season, he was selected to play in the Pro Bowl, officially confirming that he was among the best of the best.

In almost every way, Joe Ehrmann was living the dream. In fact, he was living *my* dream. Like those of many young men, all of my teenage years were ordered around the slim possibility that I might be able to play professional football. I endured two-a-day practices in the terrible summer heat and suffocating humidity. My identity in high school and the posters on my bedroom walls all centered on football.

To be a football player—a pro football player—was to be a man.

As Joe said in his popular TEDx Talk in Baltimore, the city where he made his name as a football player, culturally "we associate masculinity with athletic ability—size or strength or some sort of skill set that allows you to compete on the playground and win."

Boys who show signs of those skills are identified and elevated. They're made to be special. In other cases, if a boy is a troublemaker, parents see sports as a potential cure for what's wrong with them. "Get all that energy out on the field," they say. "Give the boy some structure." I talked to Steve Cook, the fitness icon and bodybuilder with millions of adoring fans, about what had drawn him to athletics. Turns out, it was his dad.

"I was one of seven kids growing up in Idaho, and my dad was a high school athletic director and basketball coach," he told me. Sensing that his kids needed an outlet for all their energy, Steve's father decided from the get-go that he was going to "work" the energy out of them. "From the time I was 8, 9, 10 years old, if I wanted to watch TV," Steve remembers, "I had to do 50 pushups every commercial." All Steve wanted to do was watch a little television, but you can be sure that his father thought he was helping him become a man. And you know what, Steve probably wouldn't disagree with you. "At the time, I didn't think it was nice, but you know, now I'm very grateful for that, because it was one of those things that I naturally had a capacity for and took to really well. My dad saw that and kinda pushed me into it."

Obviously, guys like Joe and Steve are grateful for being introduced to athletics. It's the central passion of their lives. Who knows where Steve or Joe would have ended up without the gym or the coaches whom they met on their journeys. But like all things when it comes to masculinity, it's not so simple. There is a darker side to it as well, specifically when boys learn simultaneously that sports are a place to excel and that their masculinity is tied to that excellence.

"That is a lie," Ehrmann says. "Being a man doesn't have a single thing to do with athletic ability."

Think about all the incredible athletes out there whose prowess on the field doesn't line up with the way they conduct their personal lives. Take Antonio Cromartie, a four-time Pro Bowler who led the entire NFL in interceptions in 2007 and holds the record for the longest play in NFL history. He is mind-bogglingly talented. But you forget all of that when you watch him in a 2010 episode of HBO's *Hard Knocks*, a sports documentary series, where he struggles to remember and recite the names of his eight children (from seven mothers), three of whom are the same age. Cromartie now has 10 children with twins on the way, and reportedly pays close to $340,000 a year in child support.

Remember Gilbert Arenas, the ultra-talented point guard for the Golden State Warriors and Washington Wizards? Not only was he a prolific scorer and a back-to-back-to-back NBA All-Star who led the entire league in minutes played during the 2005–06 season, but he and his Wizards teammate Javaris Crittenton threatened each other with handguns in the team locker room. Is that what men do? Threaten each other with dangerous weapons over a $1,100 gambling debt? This move cost Arenas $7.5 *million* in salary. Crittenton is currently serving a 23-year prison sentence on an unrelated 2015 manslaughter charge.

On the flip side, consider someone like Jason Brown, who stepped away from the NFL (and a lucrative contract) in his prime to become a farmer. Not only that, but he donates his crops to food pantries in the area. Of course, it's not just NFL players who cut against the grain of the macho athlete archetype. In the 1980s and 1990s, Manute Bol became both the tallest man to ever play in the NBA and the league's first African-born player. He was a member of the Dinka tribe from the war-ravaged country of Sudan. Manute was an incredible athlete who could play in the post like a traditional center and then drain three-pointers from well beyond the arc when given the chance. But most impressive of all is that Manute spent nearly every cent of his NBA salary from 8 years in the league helping Sudanese refugees through his own charity and countless other organizations. He made dozens of trips back and forth to Sudan—his 7-foot-7 frame folded like a lawn chair into commercial airline seats. His athlete's ego was so small, he even allowed himself to be the butt of jokes if it raised money for causes he cared about: He participated in a celebrity boxing match against William "Refrigerator" Perry; he signed a 1-day contract with a professional ice hockey team even though he'd never skated a day in his life; and once he actually dressed up as a horse jockey.

I'm reminded of the Spanish soccer player Andres Iniesta, who is routinely described as one of the best midfielders to ever play the game. On the largest stage in all of sports—the final match of the World Cup—Andres scored a goal and, rather than celebrating his own achievement, he removed his jersey to reveal a touching tribute to a fellow Spanish player who had just died of a heart attack. Andres didn't have to do that—after all, the player who died was captain of Andres's rival club, and Andres himself received a yellow card for the tribute, a big risk in the most important match of his life. The soccer world has mostly forgotten the goal itself, but they'll never forget how Andres honored a fallen player in its wake. You tell me which event makes him more of a man—his goal, or his humility and respect for his fellow players and the game itself?

I told you earlier about an important documentary called *The Mask You Live In*,[1] which many people had recommended to me after I had begun to explore the themes in this book. **The most powerful person in that documentary is none other than Joe Ehrmann. One of the things he said in the film felt like it was aimed directly at me. Speaking of his own time in the league, he said, "Football became a tremendous place to hide. You can hide inside that helmet. You can hide behind the roar of the crowd. You can project this persona—the epitome of what it means to be a man in this culture."**

It wasn't until 2007 that I realized I'd been hiding inside my helmet. It wasn't until I broke my wrist, bounced out of football, and ended up on my sister's couch that I realized how much I'd been using sports as a crutch. I had no idea what life was like. I had no serious relationships. I had a deep and abiding passion for sports, but no driving passions in my life besides winning and beating other people.

The guys who go pro are lucky in this regard. They find some fame. They make a few million dollars, which allows them to float in the bubble of the sporting life and devote themselves to the glories of game day. And when their playing days are over, they (presumably) have banked a tidy fortune to see them through. But for most guys—guys like me—there is no safety net. When their sports career ends, it's just the hard splat of reality.

Steve Cook had the same experience with what he called

"a little school tryout" with the Tennessee Titans. Everything was riding on it for Steve, but it didn't pan out. Then he fractured his ankle and made the hard choice to give up football. "It was tough because that's your identity," he recalled. "You don't think about anything else after football."

Whether it's football or baseball or soccer, at that level, it's your life. *You don't think about anything else after football.* That's a sobering statement, especially in hindsight. I remember those days in college. It was like, "Oh, I'll just keep going and see how far I can get." You're not studying. You're not maintaining any of your relationships. You're not engaged in the world around you. You don't care about class. The only reason you're going to school at all is so you can play. And then boom, one day it's over.

This is when it all comes crashing down. The thing you used for years to define your worth and measure your masculinity—your prowess on the field—now is totally useless. It no longer applies. The idea that you're only as good as you play might be motivating on the field, but off the field it's devastating. **As Joe Ehrmann put it, "Nothing is quite so painful as feeling you don't quite measure up as a man." That is exactly how athletes feel when they are no longer athletes. And men will do anything to delay that crushing feeling.**

One of the most common ways guys do this is when they play through injuries. As one sociology study of professional English soccer players found:

> *Players learn from a relatively young age to "normalize" pain and accept playing with pain and injury as part and parcel of the life of a professional footballer . . . Injured players—and in*

> *particular players with long-term injuries—*
> *may experience a loss of self-esteem and*
> *self-confidence as a result of their inability to*
> *take part in the one activity which, above all oth-*
> *ers, sustains their positive self-image.*[2]

Obviously a lot of this pressure is self-directed, but society also deserves some blame for what it celebrates and holds up as an example. When a player literally gets decleated and knocked flat, then gets back in the game, fans go crazy. But when that player seeks medical attention or takes himself out of the game, the reaction is often indifference, or worse. Players who don't play through pain, or who take too long coming back from injury, are often considered weak.

In his last years with the Chicago Bulls, Derrick Rose was regularly shredded by fans and local sports media for what they perceived as an overabundance of caution coming back from a series of right leg injuries. In September 2015, the *Chicago Sun-Times* ran an article with this headline:[3]

> *Derrick Rose has missed more games in 2 years*
> *than Tim Duncan has in his career.*

The implication of the headline—backed up by the judgmental, condescending tone of the entire article—is clear: Derrick is a fragile weakling, while Tim Duncan is a *real man*. **We don't respect self-care in men. We respect invincibility (a mask we will discuss at length later on).**

When guys lose their ability to play sports, they sometimes compensate through an obsession *with* sports.

Psychologist Martin Phillips-Hing has explained the role that sports can play in their lives:

> *I would suggest that most men watch soap operas too, except they call it sports. Think about when you most often publicly see men expressing strong emotions such as joy...fear ...disappointment...sadness...anger.* Sports, like novels and soap operas, allow men to identify and live vicariously through their team.[4]

A man's interest in sports allows him to bond with strangers in social situations and can often serve as the bedrock for certain relationships with friends and family. We root for the same teams and are joined in common cheering. We watch games together and have shared experiences because of them. These interactions can be profoundly meaningful. Many of a son's fondest memories are watching the big game with his dad. Sports create a space where it is okay for a man to express his emotions, bond with other men, and become part of a group bigger than himself.

Other men, when their days on the team are over, compensate with solo exercise. They find a home in the gym. Sadly, one of the reasons some men die earlier than women is due to overexertion in the gym. Essentially, trying to prove themselves to everyone and no one, men do more than they should and hurt themselves in the process. Dr. Marianne Legato has found that men jump into intense physical activities instead of doing them slowly and gradually. I've personally allowed my ego to get the best of me many times in this fashion. Trying to push too hard in the gym, competing against others by "lifting up" or going as hard as they do even though we aren't competitors, has been the source of numerous injuries in my own life. This is true for a lot of guys who suddenly try to prove themselves through exercise. They don't have the cardiac reserve and strength required to meet those demands, and it puts them in harm's way.[5]

When Steve Cook was going through a divorce, he went straight to the gym. "At the time, I didn't have a lot of other things feeling good in my life, and exercise releases endorphins, so I think, you know, the gym is . . ." I suspect he trailed off while telling me the story because he recognized that he'd fully retreated into his athlete mask during that time in his life.

But to finish his thought, I think he meant that the gym, like sports, is something you can control. It's a way to bang out those feelings rather than deal with them. Some guys go there, driven by insecurity or frustration, and hide from those emotions. They think a six-pack will make them feel valuable or happier. They think setting a personal-best deadlift will give them that hit of "I'm the man" that they crave and miss.

Steve and I talked about the movies we used to watch and the action heroes we idolized—Schwarzenegger, Stallone, Van Damme. Sure, they had great bodies. Sure, they could do amazing amounts of damage with their bare hands. But is that really why we admired them?

"Digging deeper into all those things," Steve went on, "even when you take those characters, what happened in most of these movies? They were serving others, and ultimately their needs came second. That is really at the core of happiness, I think. And that's at the core of all the guys in my life who I look up to."

What Steve is talking about is selflessness and sacrifice. These are virtues you learn as an athlete on a team. You learn to put your needs and goals second to the needs and goals of the team. For example, as a wide receiver, I always wanted to catch as many balls and score as many touchdowns as possible. But sometimes, the team needed me to be a good downfield blocker in the running game so as to create balance in our offense and give us a better shot to win. And, by doing my job right, I actually opened up more opportunities for me to achieve my goals. So of course I was happy to block, and to not get the ball every time. I blocked for my teammates as enthusiastically and aggressively as I ran my routes and went up for the ball. It was a symbiotic relationship where, if everyone put the needs of the team ahead of his own, everybody won.

When the team is gone and the playing days are over, however, a weird thing happens to many guys stuck behind the Athlete Mask. The value of selflessness and sacrifice starts to disappear, and all that's left is competitiveness and the need to win. This rears its ugly head for guys most often in their romantic relationships, which, ironically enough, are themselves a certain kind of team in which these virtues are just as important.

And yet, before you know it, the partner stops feeling like a teammate and starts looking more like an opponent. Everything becomes a competition. Getting your way, getting the other person to admit they were wrong, refusing to apologize unless they apologize first, *winning* arguments. These are the hallmarks of a partner hiding behind the Athlete Mask. These traits are among the hardest things for women to deal with, because my experience with the women in my life has been that they are not wired so strongly for winning at all costs.

In his legendary book, *How to Win Friends and Influence People,* Dale Carnegie has a chapter titled "You Can't Win an Argument." Most women read that title and nod their heads. Guys struggling behind the Athlete Mask read it and say to themselves, "Oh really, you wanna bet?"

This is how Dale explained it:

> You can't win an argument. You can't because if you lose it, you lose it; and if you win it, you lose it. *Why? Well, suppose you triumph over the other man and shoot his argument full of holes and prove that he is* non compos mentis. *Then what? You will feel fine. But what about him? You have made him feel inferior. You have hurt his pride. He will resent your triumph.*

Dale is talking to a male audience in a business context at a time when business was a male-dominated world. But his point is absolutely relevant to romantic relationships today. The men who understand this point are more likely to have meaningful, healthy long-term relationships. Those who don't?

Well, The Gottman Institute in Seattle, which takes a "research-based approach to strengthening relationships," has found that "the frequency and intensity of negative interactions (arguments/fights) was one of the strongest predictors of divorce."[6] In happy couples, the ratio of positive and negative interactions during a disagreement is 5:1. In relationships headed to divorce or breakup, the ratio is 0.8:1.[7]

And the source of those negative interactions? I bet Dale

Carnegie would say (and Steve Cook would agree) a big part of it is this insistent, competitive desire to win arguments. I know it's true for me. One of the big reasons the relationship that brought me out to Los Angeles unraveled so quickly is that my girlfriend and I were constantly at odds with each other. She was emotionally manipulative on her part, and I always had to get my way in every other aspect of the relationship. I could never lose an argument with her. I would keep fighting until she admitted she was wrong, or she just gave in and quit. The idea that we were on the same team, that we could *both* win, never dawned on me. Win-win, what's that?

The competitive streak that had been baked into me as an athlete made my approach to our fights second nature, but what made it worse is that I was doing it to compensate for an insane vulnerability I felt. I'd left New York City, where I had a great life, to move to Los Angeles, where I knew nobody, all for this girl. I left my happiness in those early months entirely in her hands. I felt like I was out on a high wire with no net. I could fall at any moment. *I could lose.*

Of course I didn't let my girlfriend know or see any of that. No chance! Then she'd really have me over a barrel, and I'd never get the upper hand. That's how I thought about it, hidden behind my Athlete Mask. The destructiveness of that controlling, competitive mind-set is something I learned only in the months after our eventual breakup, just as Steve Cook learned it in the months after his divorce.

I was lucky enough to talk to another Steve who had some experience with professional football. In late 2015, I met Steve Weatherford, the Super Bowl–winning punter for the New York Giants. He spent 10 years in the NFL, was a two-time All-American, and quite honestly, is one of the fittest human beings I've ever met. He and I became great friends, and I then hosted him on the School of Greatness podcast. He and I have traveled together; he's crashed at my house in Los Angeles a number of times; and we've become like brothers.

I'll tell you, there's no experience like hearing a multi-millionaire, Super Bowl champ snoring away in your living room, and then 2 hours later, hearing him wake up at 3:15 a.m. to go get a workout in, even though he is retired.

Like a lot of athletes, Steve partially took to sports because he had something he wanted to prove. He told me one of his biggest motivators was a bully who mercilessly teased him for being small. The teasing and bullying made Steve so miserable, he worked out every day over one summer break to put on 20-plus pounds of muscle. Mastering his body and mastering the playing field were ways of earning confidence and fighting back indirectly against his tormentor.

You hear a lot of stories like this in sports. **It's fine to have motivation—the problem is when this motivation is fused into our DNA and identity.** Someone like Steve comes to believe at an early age that he has to prove himself, to beat other people, if he is to have any worth or be safe, and the risk is that he'll never let go of that idea. This mindset is certainly true of countless millions of men around the world. What was so special and educational to me about my interview with Steve Weatherford was that despite the bullying in his formative years, he did *not* do that.

When I spoke with him for my podcast, he was fresh off his decision to retire. He easily could have spent another six to eight seasons in the league. He was making close to $3 million per year playing professional sports—living the dream, being an alpha male and elite athlete—and yet he walked away.

I had to know why.

Steve told me a story about the birth of his fourth child. JJ was born the day before Steve was supposed to report to training camp. He spent a few hours with his newborn and wife and then hopped on a flight to New Jersey. The flight was delayed in the air due to weather and ultimately redirected to Washington, DC. He landed and was forced to wait for a bus, but the bus never came.

Steve had never been late for a practice in his life, and he refused to start now. So he rented a car at 3:00 a.m. and began his drive to New Jersey. He was making good time, the weather was fine, and it appeared he'd make it just in time to suit up. At mile marker 58 on the New Jersey Turnpike, Steve hit an unexpected flooded patch of road at 75 miles per hour. His car hydroplaned, spun, and headed straight for a cement embankment. Knowing he would hit it, he tucked his chin and grabbed the wheel as tightly as he could. The car crashed into the concrete, flew into the air, went up and over the embankment, went across oncoming traffic, and smashed into the guardrail on the other side of the road.

He came to, shocked that he was alive, then crawled out of the back right door of his totaled red rental Jetta and called 911. As he did, another car driving northbound on the turnpike hydroplaned just as he had. It smashed into his car at more than 80 miles per hour.

Steve ran to help the other driver, whom he found slumped over the steering wheel, bleeding profusely and unresponsive. As he attempted to pull the driver out, he found all the doors refused to budge. Filled with adrenaline, Steve managed to pry open the back right door—the same one he'd managed to climb out of in his own car. Then he pulled the driver from his seat, through the car, and out the door to safety.

What does this have to do with anything? What Steve realized in that moment hit me as hard as his car must have hit that guardrail.

"The whole reason I'm telling you this story," he said, was that "after it happened, something in my mind changed, and I wasn't passionate about football anymore. I wasn't like . . . I got to get to practice on time. I just knew that football wasn't my journey anymore."

To armchair psychologize for a second, I think what happened to Steve in that moment was that his Athlete Mask was ripped clean off. Although he was never some self-obsessed jock who repressed his feelings, football and the self-worth he derived from his competitive drive were central to his identity. Think about it: Not 24 hours earlier, Steve hadn't thought twice about leaving his wife and newborn son to arrive on time at his *tenth* training camp. In fact, he'd jumped through every hoop imaginable to keep up his own imaginary streak of practice punctuality, like it was a contest. He was behaving as if he was sprinting for the finish line of a race and was going to win a medal when he walked through the front doors of the New York Giants practice facility. How many hoops do you think he would have jumped through if his wife had asked him to stay one more day? How much of a contest might he have turned that into? Probably a pretty bad one that almost certainly would have been a *must-win*. I don't know though, and Steve probably doesn't know either, because that simply wasn't an option. Football was who Steve was, just as football was who I was and who Joe Ehrmann was.

In that life-changing moment, the absurdity of it—the whole lie—became clear to Steve. Not long after that, at the end of the 2015 season, he decided it was time to hang 'em up, and so he retired. His goal? To have "impact." Not to have impact by hitting other men on the football field, but to have impact on the lives of all types of people off the field.

That might seem strange, considering the guy was a clutch player for a team that played in front of millions of people over the years. But he no longer saw football as a meaningful pursuit, nor did he believe his sports career was a way to be of service to his family and others.

"You know, it's cool to have a Super Bowl ring," he told me. "But dude, in 10 years, nobody's going to care. Nobody'll even remember my name. But they'll remember if I impact their life. That's why I'm retiring from the National Football League. I want to have a legacy. I want to have an impact."

Steve was smart with his money and saved a lot of it, so he was able to retire comfortably. But he gave me a definition of "prosperity" that I think is great.

"Prosperity," Steve said, "is a combination of health, wealth, happiness, and love. And I gravitate towards people like that, because I want that in my own life, and I want to share that with other people as well."

I pondered his words for a while. I realized that's not a bad definition of what it means to be a successful man. Heck, even a successful human being. Health, wealth, happiness, and love. *That's a man,* I thought. And being such a man has nothing to do with an NFL championship.

After Steve dropped that nugget of truth on me, he gave me a pair of tennis shoes he bought that morning as a surprise gift. Then he got up, left my house, and went off on his way to have more impact on the world.

| WHAT CAN WE DO RIGHT NOW? |

As athletes we're obsessed with how we look, with how we perform, and with winning. We're consumed by competition as the measuring stick for our manhood. But our self-worth has nothing to do with those things. It has to do with our values and principles. Specifically, our self-worth has less to do with our physical contributions to the world, and much more to do with our relationships and the positive legacy that we leave behind. Yet how many of us athletes actually *became* athletes as a defense mechanism for feeling not good enough, not smart enough, or feeling less than? How many of us spend so much time working out that we neglect other skills and emotional connections? One thing athletes avoid is going deep and getting real. I know that was me for a long time. What I needed—what got me to break through the Athlete Mask—was to find balance. You can find balance right now.

What's Available When You Drop This Mask (Athlete)

Remember Athlete Man, you are a gift, and there's so much to celebrate about you. The people who care about you the most have been waiting to see what's behind your mask. It's time to reveal the real you. These are some of the things that can flood back into your life when you drop this mask.

Creativity

Culture

New experiences

Connections with other humans

Self-worth

A healthy relationship with your image

Balance

Time to do other things you enjoy

MEN:

Balance is one of those things that is easy to consider from a distance but hard to apply and maintain. The first step is figuring out what needs to be addressed in your life that is out of balance. What have you been avoiding by focusing only on your appearance or your athletic achievements? What have you been neglecting?

Here are five core areas of your life to focus on:

1. **Health:** mental, physical, emotional
2. **Relationships:** intimate, family, friends
3. **Wealth:** finances, career, education, business
4. **Contribution:** making an impact in the world and other people's lives, being of service
5. **Spiritual:** connecting to a higher power or your spiritual beliefs

Rate yourself in each area on a scale of 1 to 10. What would a 10 look like in each area? Write this down in your journal.

What are your values and principles that you can lean on so that you can figure out how to contribute to the world, and to your own happiness, in each of these areas?

If you have no idea how to answer any of those questions, don't worry, you're not alone. The place to start is with developing your emotional intelligence, social skills, and your presence in the world outside of physical achievement and athletic accomplishment.

The goal for you is to step out of your comfort zone daily! Start reading and doing things that are intellectually stimulating. Read new books or watch new movies that you normally wouldn't see. Get involved in something with the arts, music, or dance. Do things that develop your brain and your heart and not your biceps. Choose activities that do not reinforce the Athlete Mask. For me, it was learning guitar in college, joining the school musical, and learning to salsa dance.

The more you get out of your comfort zone in these areas, the more you'll break through the Athlete Mask. Soon enough you'll become a better, balanced man.

WOMEN:

The best thing a woman can do to help a man remove the Athlete Mask is to lead by example. Have deeper conversations with him. Be open and vulnerable to show him what that looks like. Communicate those feelings that scare you, and that you think might be scaring him. To support him in creating balance in his life, create a schedule, timeline, or a list of priorities with him so that you include other things in your relationship as a team, and thus in his life.

Invite him to participate in activities he normally wouldn't be interested in. Encourage him to get out of his comfort zone by suggesting things you can do together where the protection of the Athlete Mask feels less necessary. You could volunteer at an animal shelter, for instance. There are very few things as disarming as a bunch of shelter dogs that just want to play and shower you with love.

Ultimately what he is lacking, as a result of his fear of vulnerability, is intimacy. Find ways to create the connection necessary to build intimacy. If he can drop into his heart and you can hold the space for him to practice intimacy, everyone wins.

THE MATERIAL MASK

A man's ledger does not tell
what he is, or what he is
worth. Count what is in him,
not what is on him, if you
would know what he is worth—
whether rich or poor.

—HENRY WARD BEECHER

I AM SITTING in a multimillionaire's wingback chair, in his 16-bedroom Beverly Hills mansion. By his own account, this man has lived an incredible life. His house is a long way from the doublewide trailer where he grew up, with a father in prison and a single mother who made $20,000 per year. It's a long way from 12-hour workdays on a farm or his first apartment in Los Angeles, which was just 250 square feet. It's hard to keep all the details straight as he's telling them to me, but his account has all the hallmarks of the classic rags to riches story.

Looking back on his early years, he tells me that it's hard for him to imagine having ever met anyone who would have made more than $50,000 per year. He had a few people who looked out for him: a supportive grandmother, a stepfather who helped build him a basketball court and encouraged him to play. But eventually his mother's second marriage grew rocky, then fell apart, and he was back in a broken home. He lived near the projects, so he saw kids join gangs, and he could have easily gone that way himself. Christmas was not a happy time, but a reminder of just how little he and his family had. He wasn't able to finish college—it was too expensive. He ended up moving back home with his mother with just $47 in his bank account.

Yet, here he was, not just wealthy but *conspicuously* wealthy. So conspicuously wealthy that you've probably heard of him—or rather, seen him and his expensive toys on YouTube. The man I am talking to, and about, is Tai Lopez, an Internet entrepreneur and marketer, whose videos have been viewed hundreds of millions of times.

You saw them because he wanted you to see them—he paid for you to see them with an advertising campaign that costs hundreds of thousands of dollars (someone who worked with him said even a million dollars) a month. Videos of him pulling into his garage with his Ferrari or his Lamborghini. Videos of him giving a tour of his mansion with legions of models running around half naked. Even by the exaggerated standards of Los Angeles, it was all a bit much.

The results of his steady PR blitz have been impressive. On the "About" page of his YouTube channel, we discover that he has become "an investor, partner, or advisor to over 20 multimillion-dollar businesses." His TEDx Talk has been seen more than six million times. He has well over three million followers on social media. And he does have a very nice house, I can tell you that. It's in one of the wealthiest zip codes in the world: Beverly Hills, 90210. And that was no accident.

I wanted to talk to Tai because he's a lover of books—he's read more than anyone I know. In fact, he has a free email newsletter called "Book-of-the-Day." With 1.4 million subscribers in 40 countries, he calls it one of the world's largest book clubs. I also wanted to talk to Tai because money seems so central to his lifestyle and his image, and I wanted to know what that was like. What are the best and hardest parts about Tai's luxurious lifestyle that he portrays and puts out to the world? What do people not understand about money and wealth? Is there a number he's striving for? What does it feel like to know that some people might see him as a meal ticket? **Does having money make him feel like more of a man?**

But first, out of pure personal curiosity, I just wanted to ask him a simple question: How old are you? I wasn't trying to trick him. He mentioned a pivotal moment that happened when he was 23 or 24 years old, so I asked him how old he was now to put it into context.

He told me that his publicist told him not to say. I must have asked him this question six different ways, but he just would not answer.

He joked that hiding his age was one of the masks he wore. I suppose it is, though I can't tell why. If I had to guess, I'd say he's in his early forties, which considering how young he looks and all that he's accomplished financially, is *incredibly* impressive. It just struck me as odd that he'd wear his age as a mask and odder still that he knew it was a mask.

But that's Tai. He's like a lot of guys. Complicated.

The pivotal point in Tai's life came when he met a farmer named Joel Salatin, who would go on to be a famous activist and successful entrepreneur. Tai, when he was younger, worked on Joel's farm. Joel was one of the first successful people that Tai had ever met—possibly the first millionaire he'd ever been in the same room with. Overhearing a conversation about a neighbor who wanted to rent out a cattle farm, Tai took a chance and spoke up when Joel mentioned that he liked the opportunity but was too busy to take advantage. Even though he had no money, Tai took a risk that would change his life. If Joel put up the money, Tai would put up the labor—the sweat equity. Joel agreed.

To pull it off, Tai woke up at 5:00 a.m. every day and worked until six in the evening, all while still doing his job on Joel's farm. Some nights he'd work until 10:00 p.m., grabbing just a few hours of sleep and starting the whole cycle over again. This was his life, 7 days a week. It must have been backbreaking labor. At the end of the year, Joel and Tai split the profits. Tai walked away with $12,000—a *fortune* to most young men. It's still a decent chunk of change, period.

Seeing the way Tai lit up, even years later, talking about that $12,000, I could tell what the money meant to him. Coming from a place of instability, of feeling like you aren't worth much and will never amount to

much, a payday like that—an experience like that—can change a life. It certainly did for Tai.

I understood the emotion emanating from Tai as he spoke. I grew up in a similar fashion. My family wasn't dirt poor, but we weren't doing fantastic financially. The American Dream seemed far off. I know that intoxicating effect money can have, because I saw it with my brother. I saw a good kid, a talented musician, nearly throw his entire life away to chase a few dollars selling drugs (marijuana and LSD). It ended for him in prison, with a sentence of 6 to 25 years. It nearly killed his dreams and his future. Tai wasn't someone who turned to crime—but he clearly felt addicted to turning a profit. He would spend the next few years looking for his next opportunity, trying to make his next big score.

Using his knowledge about land, he created a consulting business to help people buy farms in America. One of his early customers asked for a one-page paper of advice and told him he'd send him his normal consulting fee.

"So I did that," Tai told me, "and he wired me like $10,000 dollars for a 1-hour paper. And I was like, 'I'm gonna be an entrepreneur. This is much better.' *I made 10 grand in an hour.*"

Tai told me that the real money started coming in when he created a wealth advising firm, managing money for rich clients. That's where the six-figure paydays came in, and that's what he used to create his empire of Internet companies and establish the lifestyle he's famous for today.

His first big purchase was a Maserati, the Italian luxury sports car with the trident emblem on the grill. Tai wasn't ready to show it off—he just posted one photo on Facebook, he told me—but that was the inception of the Jay

Gatsby-like character we now know as Tai Lopez, Internet millionaire and motivational speaker.

I've always wanted to be financially free and make enough money to do the things I love in life. I think that desire motivates a lot of the people who have found success in business. Unlike many of my peers, I've never been one to flash my money around—maybe it's my Midwestern roots, I don't know—so Tai's mindset is interesting to me. I've never wanted a Ferrari. Even though I can afford a luxury car like that, I drive a 1991 Cadillac that I bought for $4,000 from a mentor. But still, I've been incredibly motivated by entrepreneurial accomplishments. I've wanted things that were hard to buy with money—the right connections, the label of "successful entrepreneur." I've wanted to be a *New York Times* bestselling author and an Olympian. I've wanted these things because I thought they would say something about me as a person. I thought they would make me an impressive man.

A huge portion of this drive is evolutionary. For much of human history, a man's ability to provide determined all of his prospects in life. Before money, it was literally bringing home the bacon. The guy who had the most resources was the most attractive. As a result, he was the most powerful, the most important, the most manly.

Tai described the dangers of money quite well. He said, "I think that if you're not careful, money is like a pit bull. A pit bull can save your life or it can turn around and kill you."

Think of the Walter White character in *Breaking Bad*. When Gus Fring famously asks him, "What does a man do?" Walter replies:

And a man, a man provides. And he does it even
when he's not appreciated, or respected, or
even loved. He simply bears up and he does it.
Because he's a man.

In the show, it's clear that both characters deeply believe in this idea—that a man has to financially provide for his family. As they say it, the audience is supposed to nod its head in agreement. This solemn duty that was thrust upon them by fate and by birth, that they've agreed to fulfill as the heads of their families, is supposed to make it harder for us to judge them as the murderous drug dealers they've become. Sure, they both destroy their own families in their misguided effort to "provide," but sometimes a man has to do what a man has to do, right? (This example is a vivid reminder of Victor Hugo's proverb: "Adversity makes men, and prosperity makes monsters.")

Hey, I'm not judging. I nodded right along with everyone else. Because I *get* that feeling. And I don't even have a family. At my lowest moment, I was essentially homeless, living on my sister's couch because I had no money. I know what that kind of poverty feels like, and it does not feel good.

I think people born with money, or people to whom money and material things have come easily, often forget this. It's easy for them to have a blasé attitude about money or say that it's not important to them. They've never gone hungry, or literally stuffed free bread and crackers from networking events in their pockets to take home and eat later like I did . . . or scrounged for coins in the cushions of their couch so they could order something off the dollar menu.

"There's been a lot of research on unhappy people who get wealthier, who don't get more unhappy or more happy,"

Tai said. With money, "your happiness doesn't change. But I will tell you, not having enough money is very stressful . . . the lack of money and resources is the root of all evil. And people who become crazy once they get money, mark my words, if you had met them 10 years before, they were probably crazy too." That was one of the things that Tai was very adamant about—he hates the idea that money is "poisonous."

Depending on how you define "crazy," I don't think Tai was necessarily wrong. The dominant emotion I felt when I didn't have money was shame and uncertainty. I felt like I'd let myself down, that I'd let my parents down, or that I was worthless compared to other people. When I saw a nice car drive by, I would feel that shame all over again because I could barely afford to eat. **Shame and uncertainty are only a few short steps away from depression and anxiety. Separately or together, those emotions can drive you to the brink. They can blot out everything else in your life and literally make you crazy.**

What am I doing wrong? Are all these people better than me? I'd think. Money doesn't determine worth, but it would be silly and dishonest to say that money doesn't matter at all. Of course it does. You can't exist efficiently in modern society without money or material items. I wouldn't do well without my iPhone, nor would I want to live paycheck to paycheck, wondering how I'm going to afford my next meal. But at the same time, money does not matter in the way men are taught that it does.

Most guys who feel that shame and anxiety attempt to compensate for it. I was no different. Because I felt so low, I would fantasize that someday I would be rich. My wealth would mean that I finally

mattered. I could rest easy knowing that I could afford to live up to my obligations as a man, and not be a burden on my family or anyone else. Thankfully, that shame is gone today. However, I can envision a scenario in which if I had not tried hard to improve myself, read some of the books I've read, or spoken to the incredible mentors I've learned from, I would still be primarily driven by that shame and unworthiness. Even though I've made good money and had my share of success, I would still be driven by the desire to prove to people that I was not that poor kid I once was.

I suppose that's why a lot of guys either love or hate Tai Lopez. Some see him as a hero. They want to drive nice cars. They want to be surrounded by models in their enormous mansions. They want to be able to hang out with celebrities who come over to their house. They want to be—or *appear to be*—the opposite of the invisible, ashamed, anonymous person they might feel themselves to be. Other guys see him as a fraud or a liar. They are convinced he's making it all up and that he doesn't actually have any money. They obsessively produce videos that question whether Tai rents his exotic cars or if his house is really his. If I had to guess why those doubters are so obsessed, it's because, if Tai's story is true, then deep down, they don't think they would be able to do the same things Tai has done. And that kind of self-doubt, especially to a man raised in our current culture, is too crippling not to project outward onto others.

The comments online about the interview I did with Tai are a perfect microcosm of this split opinion about him. From the more than 500 podcast episodes I've done, they are the most heated. Commenters either want to be Tai because they think he is better than them and they can learn from him, or they feel like they have to discredit him because they don't think he is better than them. Some hate him so much they get mad *at me* for interviewing him because I'm somehow giving him a platform that legitimizes him. Some have even unsubscribed from my podcast because I associated with Tai.

Regardless of which side of the aisle you sit on, however, it is hard to deny that Tai wears a version of the Material Mask. After all, this is a man who has given an MTV *Cribs*-style video tour of his vast Beverly Hills home complete with Lamborghinis, Ferraris, pool, gym, basketball court, boxing gym, movie theater, and private chef, while claiming that the video is not materialistic "even though some of you might perceive it that way." And you know what, I would have probably agreed with him at one point, except he does the same thing with the stuff he should be most proud of: *his ideas.* When he talks about what he considers the most important thing in his life—knowledge by way of books—it's almost always framed around how many new books he *bought* or how many bookshelves he had to have installed. Or he shows you how he uses $100 bills as bookmarks.

This is where the Material Mask so often gets in men's way. Wearing this mask compels you to highlight things that are not beneficial to your ability to establish real, lasting self-worth. Curating these superficial trappings requires time and energy that you could otherwise use to cultivate the real you hiding behind the Material Mask. Tai has good ideas; he has *great* ideas. If you truly listen to him, you'll hear his version of wisdom, insight, tips, and hacks that many other great thought leaders have talked about and agreed with. He has talked about the very same subjects I cover in *The School of Greatness*, for instance, and I agree with many of his theories. But here's the thing: To listen to Tai is to watch his YouTube videos. And to listen to his insight is to watch him dispense it from the captain's chair of a private jet surrounded by models in bandage dresses. Or from backstage at a concert. Or poolside at a private villa. Or in his giant Beverly Hills mansion. This extra bit of detail is like theater or a costume, and without it, it's almost like he thinks his ideas will have less value. Or worse, they won't matter. It's like the material wealth is proof that his ideas are good— and thus *he* is good—even though both are obviously good on their own merits.

The irony is, for so many people, all that materialism invalidates the quality of a person's ideas. There's nothing Tai can do to get those people to hear him, which just drives him further behind the Material Mask. It's like someone trying to convince you that they care about you by screaming, "I love you!" louder and louder right in your face at the top of their lungs with the veins bulging out of their neck. You don't hear the words; you only see the vulgar display.

Let me be clear: I'm not being critical or condescending to guys who do this. I get it. God knows, I've done stuff like this myself. I've found myself inside the same mask that Tai wears: flashing my shoe game on Instagram or taking sunset pictures of West Hollywood from my balcony or Snapchatting from my first-class seat on the way to some exotic foreign country. I've done all those things multiple times just in the course of writing this book. I have engaged with the world from behind the Material Mask. Why? Honestly, it feels good when it's on. You literally feel like a million bucks. And I would not think twice about it if I thought this kind of bragging ever made people feel good, but I know it doesn't. It's a kind of endless competition that never, ever has a finish line. Does the thinking go that the good stuff says something about you as a person, as a man? It cuts both ways. It also means that the nicer, fancier, more expensive stuff that other people have says something about them, and it says something about you in relation to them.

I'll give you an example:

I complimented Tai on his amazing house. I tried to say something like, "This must be one of the nicest houses in all of Beverly Hills." His immediate response wasn't to accept the compliment or look around and appreciate just how far he'd come and how blessed his life was. Instead, he compared himself to someone else.

"Let me tell you," Tai said, "this is nothing." He turned to his cousin, who was with him, and mentioned a house they'd recently been to with the singer Lady Gaga. It was the home of billionaire Ron Burkle, a guy who has his own jet and is a personal friend of Bill Clinton. "Wooh!" Tai exclaimed. "This is Ron Burkle's bathroom."

He said this as if to say, "I'm not that amazing in comparison to people more successful than me." But it came off as though Tai believes material possessions really say something about who you are and what you measure yourself against, and even someone who has a 16-bedroom mansion in one of the most exclusive neighborhoods in the world becomes nothing compared to the owner of an even bigger mansion, even though most people have never heard of him.

A friend of mine, Ryan Holiday, has a line in his book *Ego Is the Enemy* to this effect: "Whatever success you're after, keep in mind that someone has already had it, hated it, and deluded themselves into thinking that just a little more would solve their problems."

Another fan favorite guest interview on my podcast is with Alanis Morissette. Alanis has sold 60 million records and toured all over the planet. She has been a famous singer-songwriter for more than 2 decades now. She's made a lot of money, and she's become famous. Yet she pointed out how worthless all that is:

> *A lot of people, I think, chase fame to get the attachment stuff they never got. It's literally eyeballs looking at you, people wanting to touch you, people wanting to be near you, people being obsessed with you. What's that if not what a mother offers us or a caregiver offers us when we're born, ideally? So there's that whole conversation. Then there's just I'll get my dad's approval finally.*

Insecure people can be forgiven for thinking that fame will finally make them feel loved and whole. I think one of the big reasons why men, specifically, chase money and fame is because they were turned away earlier from those feelings of acceptance and attachment, and they found some security in this myth that being rich, that having Tai's house, will finally make them feel like men.

I like having nice things myself, and there's nothing wrong with wanting them or having them. But they are not the things that leave me fulfilled inside at the end of the day, and they don't solve all my problems once I have them.

"The money and the cars . . ." Alanis said to me. "It's to what end? What does this actually provide you personally in your soul, in your heart? And I think that's where it gets a little dangerous, chasing attention. Whether it's relevance or fame or whatever it is."

So many men find themselves doing this today—just as they have for thousands of years. *If I make this money, I'll be important. If I make this money, my parents will respect me. If I make this money, I can get a pretty wife. If I make this money, it makes me a real man.*

Is that really what success is supposed to be? Fraught with all this anxiety? Is happiness supposed to be the carrot in front of the donkey—always in our sights, but always out of reach?

There's a line from Albert Einstein: "Try not to become a man of success, but rather try to become a man of value." This advice is similar to something Alanis expressed to me. I asked her how she dealt with the fact that success—money and fame—comes and goes in the music industry. She said it's essential to have the proper definition of what success is for you, and that it should not be materialistic. For her, success is the ability to express herself musically (which makes sense considering the profession she chose). She said:

> For me, if I have a sense of self, I'm in my seat, as
> I call it, and I'm being expressed, I'm being of

service, and I'm taking care of myself so that I
don't burn out, that is the definition of success
for me. And then I have to start having some per-
sonal fulfillment, too, because I had profes-
sional fulfillment nonstop, and I still have that.

I love that.

One last Tai story. Tai said something to me about money that I agreed with—that it's not the money that matters but how one spends it.

"There's two ways you can consume, as a person making money," he said to me. "There's conspicuous consumption and inconspicuous. And conspicuous is what makes you unhappy. So I don't have any nice watches, okay? And some of my friends are like, 'You should have a Rolex because if you are successful, you need to show that.' Well, I don't really care about watches, never did. So if I bought a watch for myself, it would be what's called conspicuous, me trying to show off."

I thought that was a very self-aware and intelligent thing to say. As he said it, and as his words registered in my memory, all I could think of was the famous Beatles song that reminds us what money can't buy—love. It never has, and it never will. **We're all going to do different things with our money. We're all going to have different numbers that we aspire to reach. But at the end of the day, if you think that any amount of money will make you accepted by other people, or will get you friends, you're doing it for the wrong reasons and you are fooling yourself.**

Sure, you might be able to pay for a seat at an exclusive

dinner table . . . but you can't make anyone sitting around it actually like you. **You cannot purchase connection. And your net worth will never create self-worth, no matter how much the two might seem to be related.**

Sitting down with Tai reminded me of a conversation I had with Tony Robbins, because my conversation with Tony was the opposite of my conversation with Tai in almost every way. Tony is a rich dude, no question about it. He's rich enough to fly around on a private jet (in fact, one of the interviews I did with him was on his private jet as it idled on the runway). He wrote a book called *Money: Master the Game*. During my interview with him for the launch of that book, he told me that his companies are now worth billions of dollars but that the big breakthrough in his life had nothing to do with achieving that kind of material success. It was not going from making $38,000 a year to $1 million per year. It wasn't, after being stuck at $1 million per year for seven straight years, even as he helped more and more people get healthier and wealthier, finally breaking through and making $3 million per year and then much, much more than that. His big *a-ha!* moment came when Sir John Templeton, the famous mutual funds pioneer, told him that he'd never seen anyone tithe 10 percent of what they earned for at least a decade who didn't become "incredibly financially free." Tony's whole life changed when he figured that out—when he started giving instead of trying to receive.

The lesson hit home like a thunderbolt one day early in Tony's career while he sat in an all-you-can-eat restaurant in Marina Del Rey, California. He was building his business, but like all new endeavors, there were some fits and starts, some ups and downs. He happened to be in the middle of one of those downs. He was down to his last $25 or so. He was broke enough that he walked to the restaurant from Venice Beach instead of driving to save on gas.

As he was finishing his meal, he watched a beautiful woman walk in to eat with her young son. The little boy was wearing a three-piece suit—with a vest! He was polite and mature. Like a gentleman, he pulled the chair out for his mother to sit. Tony was struck by the love and care that this little boy had for his mom. And so, after he paid for his meal, he walked up and introduced himself.

As Tony was telling me this story—decades later—I could see the emotion he felt. Tony is a big guy, and yet he was tearing up in front of me about the memory.

"I said, 'Hi,' I think he said his name was Ronny, and I said, 'Ronny, you're a class act. I saw you open the door for your lady, I saw you hold out the chair for your lady.' He goes, 'She's my mom.' I said, 'That's even more classy.'"

Tony commended him for taking his mom out to lunch. The kid looked at him with a serious face the way young kids do who haven't learned how to joke around yet, and he said, "I'm not really taking her to lunch. I'm just 11 and I don't have a job."

Without even thinking about it, Tony gave the kid all the money in his pocket—basically all he had left in the world—so he could take his mother out to lunch. Then he walked out of the restaurant and went on with his life.

Think about that: Tony had no money, no way to pay his rent, and he was going to have to consider going hungry for his next several meals. Yet he was euphoric. He told me he basically *flew* home, he felt so proud of himself.

The next day, he checked his mail and found a letter

from a guy he'd been hounding about a business transaction for *months,* who hadn't returned his calls. In the letter was a check for $1,000 plus interest, and an apology.

Tony began to cry. How could something like that happen? Were the two events related? He told me he decided that they were:

> *I don't know if it's true, but I decided that day that this happened because I did the right thing. Because I didn't have a plan, it wasn't a strategy, I always felt this little soul beside me, I knew what was right, and I did it. I didn't do it because I thought I could or I couldn't, I didn't even think about it,* and that's the day I became a wealthy man, because I still didn't have any money, but scarcity left my body. *I've had plenty of ups and downs since that time, but I never went back to that fearful mindset of, "Oh my God, how's it going to happen?"*

To me, what Tony is describing is life after the Material Mask has been removed. He is painting a picture of what it feels like, as a man, to live beyond scarcity, to live free—to value yourself, your work, your ideas, independent of how others may see them.

As I thought about this idea, and as I reflected on the moment where I first encountered it, it struck me that Tony was telling me this story of deep humility from a captain's chair in his private jet. In this respect, it was not unlike any number of Tai's videos. I understand that both men probably fly private jets because of convenience, but when Tai does it, it seems more like a status indicator. At least that's what it feels like. I don't actually know; it's simply the perception each man has created around himself by the choices he has made throughout his adult life. And I think that is exactly the point. When Tony talks, you hear his story and his ideas. When Tai talks, you see the plane and the models in bandage dresses. You won't hear about Tai's service, like the humanitarian award he won for his contributions to the Heifer Project, because that's not what he shines the spotlight on. If the online comments for my interview with Tai are any indication, I am not alone in having that impression.

If you have ever attended one of Tony's magical and life-changing Date with Destiny events—or watched the Netflix documentary about it—you'll see a packed house hanging on Tony's every word, and you'll see Tony himself, up there on stage in black pants or black shorts and an untucked black shirt. He doesn't stay up on stage removed from the crowd; he climbs down and gets in there with his audience. Basically, he's just himself. He's comfortable in his own skin, and he's comfortable letting the power of his message and his ideas speak for themselves and stand on their own.

That, to my mind, is what a happy, fulfilled man looks like when he has removed his Material Mask. As Orison Swett Marden, one of the first great self-help writers, expressed it, "This is the test of your manhood: How much is there left in you after you have lost everything outside of yourself?" For Tony, it's clear there was a lot there. There is a lot there for Tai too. He just has to believe it. He has to believe that he will pass that test. I honestly believe Tai can get there, just as I believe any man who struggles with this issue can get there. But I don't think a man can make that happen until he sufficiently wrestles with the Material Mask that has protected him the whole time he has worn it.

| WHAT CAN WE DO RIGHT NOW? |

The road to freedom from the Material Mask is not an easy one, because at the end of the road is a healthy sense of self-worth, and that has always been a difficult issue for men in our culture. This issue is so hard because we have been taught to attach our self-worth to what we have and what we do, to our possessions, our roles in life, and our bank balances. **What we need to realize is that we are valuable, regardless of what we have. We need to recognize that, while living behind the Material Mask, there will never be such a thing as "enough" when it comes to a sufficient sense of self-worth as a man.** This means that what it all comes down to is *gratitude*!

What's Available When You Drop This Mask (Material)

Remember Material Man, you are a gift, and there's so much to celebrate about you. The people who care about you the most have been waiting to see what's behind your mask. It's time to reveal the real you. These are some of the things that can flood back into your life when you drop this mask.

Fulfillment

Worthiness

Inner peace

Attracting people who are interested in who you are, not how much you have

Feeling enough

Satisfaction with your achievements

Gratitude

MEN:

Live in gratitude. Someone who is grateful for what he has, no matter how little it is, will be more open to living a joyful life. When we live in gratitude, life gives us more to be grateful for. The practice of gratitude alleviates the constant pressure a man feels to make more, and it can ease the burden of his struggles behind the Material Mask.

The man armored by the Material Mask is attached to his results. When he achieves successful results, he feels like a winner, but when he experiences unsuccessful results, he feels like a loser. You need to remember that you are not a winner based on your results; you are a winner based on a combination of things, the most important of which are your values and contributions. An insecure and unhappy man who achieves material success will remain insecure and unhappy.

We are all gifts. When you see someone filled with love and joy, it is contagious. It doesn't matter how much money they have; what matters is how they show up in the world.

Personally, I start and end each day with the practice of gratitude, and I try to be grateful during as many moments as I can in between. As someone who grew up defensive, aggressive, and in scarcity, I realize I can quickly go back to that place of fear in a moment. And when I do, only bad things happen in my life. So by cultivating gratitude as much as possible, I feel like I'm creating magic in my life and turning dirt into gold.

Here is what you can do to practice gratitude on a daily basis. I do many of these myself, and you can start them right now:

1. When you wake up, take out your journal and write down three things for which you're grateful.
2. Before you go to sleep, ask the last person you talk to three things they are most grateful for from the day, and in reply tell them what you are grateful for from the day too.
3. My voicemail message asks people to share what they are most grateful for when they leave a message. Feel free to copy the idea.
4. Start meetings with your team or business partners with a moment that allows everyone to share what they are grateful for.
5. Acknowledge people daily with a few words that express what you're grateful for about them.

These are all ways to cultivate an attitude of gratitude that, in turn, will bring more joy into your life and will open you up to greater relationships in your life.

WOMEN:

The next time the man in your life shows his Material Mask, lean in. To help him stop hiding behind this mask, it's important to highlight the intangible, priceless characteristics he possesses that are as important, or more important, to you. One of the ways you can do this is by acknowledging the things you are most grateful for about the men in your life.

You can note personal traits like a sense of humor, kindness, empathy, selflessness, and presence—all those things you can't put a dollar value on. The journey to positive self-worth is a long one, so letting him know how valuable he is in nonmaterial ways will truly help your man to give up his reliance on the Material Mask as you walk with him along this path.

THE SEXUAL MASK

A man's need to conquer women
actually reveals a tremendous
helplessness that has made
suckers out of them for
thousands of years.

—ROBERT GREENE

NEIL STRAUSS IS a name that, for a lot of American men, is spoken with awe and reverence. At some point during the last 10 years, these men have held a book by Neil that features a black cover and binding, a red ribbon inside, and a glitzy gold edge. The book has the weight, feel, and look of the Bible—and for millions of modern men, it *is* a bible. The book is called *The Game: Penetrating the Secret Society of*

Pickup Artists, and it teaches men how to meet and hook up with women. It teaches them the superpower of sex.

Neil is the undisputed master of picking up women. For instance, one day he found himself in the middle of a "sexual free-for-all." He's in Paris, in a swinger's club, surrounded by beautiful women who, just by being there, signal they are down for pretty much anything.

"I just want a cock in me," one woman says to him, just as casually as if she's discussing the weather or politics. Briefly, he's intrigued. I mean, it'd be hard for most guys not to be. Neil describes the scene in his book *The Truth*:

> *This is the kind of woman I fantasized about as a teenager: an indiscriminate one. And more than anything I've experienced so far, this seems like free sex—because there's no spiritual baggage, drug baggage, or even much relationship baggage around it. In fact, there's no baggage or encumbrances whatsoever, just randomly intersecting body parts.*[1]

And yet, as fun and free as his time at the club is, it is also the beginning of a slow-motion train wreck. Once he is back in the States, he moves in with three—yes, three—girlfriends. Chaos ensues. Instead of sleeping on silk sheets with all these beauties, he is on the couch. There's tension, jealousy, anger, fighting, and yelling—it's all a bit too much to handle. And that doesn't even get into the self-doubt and self-loathing he feels on top of it. As he puts it, **"When I imagined living in a freewheeling love commune during my monogamous relationship, I thought I'd be**

adrift in a blissful sea of pleasure, excitement, and feminine energy. But instead I only feel embarrassed that I'm monopolizing three hearts." Neil was living what many guys would consider the ultimate dream, and it turned out to be an intense nightmare.

That time on the couch was the brief period just before it all fell apart—in a massive way. There were painful exits, an axe-wielding jealous ex, broken hearts and spirits, and, at the bottom of it all, a crushed and confused Neil.

When Neil began writing *The Game,* he was, by his own admission, a sexual amateur. Worse than that, he was what he calls an AFC (average frustrated chump). The story is his introduction to the secret society of "pickup artists"—men who make finding and sleeping with lots of women their primary purpose in life, *like a game.* Strauss told his editor that he wanted to write about this community because it was interesting. In reality, he was tired of being alone and feeling like a loser. At one sad point in his life, Neil had even considered finding a mail-order bride. He tells the story of having been on the road with the band Mötley Crüe for a book he was writing and not even getting a kiss from a single girl. By almost every definition of what it means to be a "man" in America, Neil felt like a failure and was *less* than guys who were having lots of sex.

So Neil decided he would write a book about pickup artists as a way to learn about how to meet women. He not only became a pickup artist himself, but because he is brilliant, funny, and well-spoken, he became the greatest pickup artist in the world. Then he became a kind of pickup artist guru: He built a program to teach other men what he knew, training men in the art of finding and seducing women.

By the time the book was published and took off, he had money, charm, looks, and everything his childhood-self thought was important—including the ability to seduce pretty much any woman his heart desired. He slept with scores of women, sometimes two or three at the same time, and fulfilled every fantasy he'd ever had. He was not just *a man,* he was *The Man.* He became a rock star without ever having to pick up the guitar.

I know what most guys are thinking right now. They're thinking, *"Awesome.* I want that too." You might *think* that, but you're wrong, trust me. I've been in long-term relationships, and I've been single, talking to a handful of women at the same time. There were times in my twenties when it seemed like I had a new date every night of the week. It was fun and interesting, at least for a while, but it took a lot of energy to manage so many people's emotions, and ultimately it was pretty unfulfilling. For Neil, it wasn't awesome at all. Sleeping with all of those women didn't fulfill him the way he thought it would. He'd struggled so hard to fix what he thought was "less" about him, and yet he felt empty and hollow.

It reminds me of an exchange on season five of *Mad Men.* Don Draper comes into Roger Sterling's office, dissatisfied and upset with the direction of the company. He's questioning the industry altogether, despite the luxurious office in the Madison Avenue skyscraper with all the perks. Don Draper asks Roger, "Why do we do this?" as he pours himself a drink in the middle of the morning. Roger's answer is classic, but sad. "For the sex," he says, "but it's always disappointing."

If we're honest, for so many men, life has become a

never-ending trophy hunt, but none of them end up actually feeling like a winner. We just think we've won because we've added another woman to our tally. It's not about intimacy—it's about arithmetic. And yet the math always turns out to be disappointing.

It's not just disappointing for the man, by the way. As exhausting and futile as the approach is for men, think about what it must be like for the women who are chased and objectified—seen as nothing more than notches in a bedpost to the guy she might have been genuinely interested in. A woman definitely isn't getting the best of this man, even if the guy thinks he's doing it all to please her . . . because really he's just trying to please a part of his ego.

Chris Lee, a brilliant transformational coach whom I referenced in a previous chapter, is one of the people I admire most on these subjects. More than 3 years ago, I started doing work with Chris to deal with my own masks and struggles with masculinity. Today, when he and I talk about these issues, he cuts to the core in a no-excuses, no-holds-barred way that always helps me.

On my podcast he gave a great description of how this posturing starts:

> Every boy in America learns by the time they're in junior high school to associate masculinity with issues of sexual conquest. What's it mean to be a man? It means you can bring some young girl alongside of yourself and then use her. *Use her to either gratify some kind of physical need, or use her to validate some kind of masculine insecurity. That*

certainly does not make you a man—it makes you a user of other human beings.

For most boys, junior high and high school is a time when they struggle to figure out sex, have sex, and then brag about having had sex. What's left out of the discussion is what's happening to them—and to their partners—during all of that. Boys simplify the discussion of sex down to a binary system—whether they have or haven't had it—and their social status and masculine security hang on the answer.

This mindset probably does not sound particularly shocking to most people. It's a theme in practically every high school coming-of-age movie Hollywood has produced in the last 50 years. Every after school special and TV show I watched growing up that featured school-age children eventually had an episode dealing with the anxiety of sex, virginity, and peer pressure. And that emotional cocktail doesn't just dry up at high school graduation either. It continues well into college.

That was certainly my experience. I always thought about sex in high school. I might even have obsessed about it. I wanted it so badly, but I had no clue what I was doing and was nervous about being made fun of if I didn't perform well. I'm not sure if every teen boy goes through this, but I couldn't control the amount of blood that rushed to my penis any more than I could control the desire for candy and sweets. (And I used to eat sweets all the time, every day.) I had to deceptively walk around with my shirt untucked (at my private school this wasn't allowed with our dress code) and with my books covering my front because I couldn't control the erection I always had. I remember during freshman year there was a senior, one of the best-looking girls in school, who was always flirting with me. One day she wanted to take me out to her car to have sex with me (a typical high school story, right?). I remember being so sexually excited, yet terribly afraid at the same time. I remember thinking, "This is my chance. I'm going to finally get some action *and* with an upperclassman!" But I was too afraid and embarrassed, so I awkwardly walked away, nervous out of my mind.

I had a couple of girlfriends throughout high school, and I always wanted to have sex with them if they would have wanted to. But they didn't, and as time passed, I made the conscious decision that I was going to wait until I was 18 to have sex. My three older siblings all lost their virginity by 16 or earlier, and I wanted to wait until I was a legal adult to make that decision.

It turns out, this was similar to Neil's experience too. The man who would go on to become the greatest seducer in the world—the man who taught millions of men how to get laid—spent a big chunk of his adolescence being anxious about why he wasn't having sex. As he told me in our interview:

> So what happens is you go through puberty at age 13, and then for the next 8 years in my case, there's this thing that can make you a man, but you don't own it or possess it. Someone else either has to give it to you or share it with you, and the longer you don't get it, the less of a man you feel like. I remember my friend, who was like my only friend in school, we called

ourselves the "v-club" because we were both vir-
gins. The whole experience created this incredi-
ble gulf between me and women, and me and
manhood, and it built up this huge desire.

In 2007, psychologists from New Mexico State University and the University of Houston published an article in
The Journal of Men's Studies titled "The Relationship
between Masculinity Ideology, Loneliness, and Separation-
Individuation Difficulties."[2] Their findings echoed what
would eventually be Neil's defining experience as it related
to sex. **In the article, the authors recognized that col-
lege-age men, especially in fraternities, who failed to
meet the stereotypical definitions of masculinity (men
kind of like Neil) were more likely to turn to more negative forms of male socialization in order to play
catch-up in the male world. That meant binge drinking, fighting, and casual sex with lots of partners.**

**The problem with this—besides the obvious risk of
disease or enraged exes—is if you don't get past this
phase, you end up just feeling empty. Or worse, you get
stuck in the cycle.**

Having trained himself to find and seduce women of all
types, Neil, at a certain point, found he couldn't stop himself. If he saw a woman on an airplane, he sized her up and
pondered the odds of jumping into bed with her. If he was in
a relationship, he strayed. Sex dominated his thoughts,
muscling out everything else.

Hitting rock bottom, losing the woman he loved, was,
for him, the start of the search for answers. He checked
himself into a facility that treats sex addicts and began a
path that would lead him to completely rewire his brain and

reboot the operating system that controlled all of his urges. And what resulted, as he told me, was some *truth:* His Sexual Mask had taken over his life and had wrecked it. He recalled:

> *What I thought was freedom really wasn't freedom. The freedom was in the commitments. But if you think about it, "Okay I'm gonna be single or unattached, or I'm just gonna be able to do whatever I want,"* it's like a bird that's not able to land; it gets exhausting. And going through the processes, by which I was actually able to kind of get rid of my baggage and be intimate in a relationship and not feel trapped, just opened up everything.

There are times when my podcast ends up becoming a kind of pseudo-counseling session just for me. Sometimes, this makes me nervous. (Would you want *your* therapy broadcast to millions of people?) But other times, I think it brings out the most valuable content I've ever produced. In my conversation with Neil Strauss, we hit on not only some of the deepest, most sensitive issues men face, but issues that I have struggled with intensely for the last few years.

He had caught me at a particularly appropriate time. Remember that this book opened with the story of the tour for my first book. I had just broken up with my longtime girlfriend, in part because what I thought I wanted was unlimited freedom from any and all constraints, including the sexual ones. I was now a bestselling author and had a seven-figure business—did I really want to commit my life to just one woman?

Settling down in a relationship? That has the word *settle* in it. Who wants to settle? If you're good looking, charismatic, confident—no matter your orientation—you're going to have options, and it's going to be hard to pass them up. Whether it's Tinder or Grindr, a hot body is just a swipe away.

That's what I thought I wanted. With more accomplishments, financial success, and reaching a level of age maturity, I noticed more and more women giving me attention and making themselves available. I was constantly thinking about "the next best thing." The UFC fighter Brendan Schaub explained that dilemma well to me. He said, "I feel like I'm Bruce Wayne and I have this curse . . . and the curse is options." This was and still is a struggle for me. It's like a dance where I have to make sure I'm staying grounded so that I don't trip up and fall into a destructive place.

For a little while, during my book's success, I enjoyed the perks of being single. Yet each morning on my book tour, the feelings of doubt I told you about in the beginning of this book would creep up on me: What am I doing? Why am I missing my ex? If I can't be *without* her, then why can't I be *with* her either? I suddenly understood what Neil meant when he talked about the exhausted bird that couldn't land. **The bird wasn't exhausted because it never stopped flying from nest to nest; it was exhausted because it spent all its energy staying aloft while it debated which direction to fly. Was this really what freedom is supposed to feel like?**

That's the other part of what Brendan said to me. Girls, he said, were his Bane, as in the villain in *Batman*. That drive for more, more, more, was an exhilarating challenge, but it was also the *bane* of his existence. He even called it his "addiction."

The reason I wanted to talk to Neil Strauss wasn't just because he had written books about these topics—it's because I felt like he had suffered in some of the same ways I had, and in the same ways that, I think, so many other men suffer in silence about these issues. And he had suffered. He opened up to me about the relationship with his then girlfriend, and how hitting rock bottom prompted him to figure out all of his issues:

> I cheated on Ingrid, who's my wife now, and I felt horrible. I thought I was a good guy. I really loved her, I wanted to be with her, and I cheated on her, and I just couldn't understand why would I do that to someone? Why would I hurt somebody like that who loves me? Why would I break her heart? Why would I ruin my future? And why would I act outside my ethics system and outside my morals and just for sex that wasn't even that good anyway?

Those are good, tough questions. Questions I think many men struggle with. I know I did. And they are also the questions we do our best to avoid answering. **If we're honest with ourselves, we'll admit that questions about how sex fits with our moral and ethical systems just aren't on the table. You're more likely to fit in with other guys if you put those issues to the side and talk about your sexual conquests instead. If you want to talk about feelings or love or whether your sex life is really a positive experience for everyone involved, forget about fitting in.** If the lion's share of the studies on this subject are to be believed, guys fear that revealing these struggles about intimacy is how they end up getting labeled as gay, or feminine, or a pussy. It doesn't matter what your sexual orientation is; no man wants to be talked about in a derogatory way.

So what ends up happening is sort of predictable: This very powerful force in our lives is left unexamined. We fall into and out of relationships, into and out of sexual partners, and we barely take stock. Add to that the especially powerful effect of pornography—which is now more readily available than water—and you have a recipe for a boiling cauldron of issues.

There is a darkness there, in a lot of guys. Matthew Hussey, *New York Times* bestselling author of *Get the Guy* and one of the world's leading dating experts for women (that is, he helps women meet men), points out just how aggressive a lot of guys are about sex. Think even about the words we use—like "conquest"—to describe what is supposed to be an experience rooted in mutual pleasure. Matthew broke it down for me when we talked at his home in Los Angeles:

> *If you watch porn these days, it is dispropor-*
> *tionately aggressive. It's all about dominating*
> *women, so much of it is about humiliation. It's*
> *not just the amount of sex. Guys feel more like*
> *a man if they're dominating and aggressive in*
> *bed. Instead of the definition of a man being*
> *about making her feel good in bed, it's all about*
> *showing physical dominance over her. Because*
> *that is so pervasive in porn, I think men have a*
> *warped sense of reality when it comes to mas-*
> *culinity in the bedroom. I dread to think about*

> *kids who are like 9 or 10 who have never kissed*
> *a girl and that is their first data point with sex,*
> *that that's what it looks like. It's creating some*
> *messed-up men.*

For Neil, the issues were deeper. He had a lot of child-hood struggle to work through:

> *I started to sort of learn about what unknown,*
> *unconscious hidden forces were operating on*
> *me that made me make this decision. Largely,*
> *having a depressed, controlling mother and*
> *parents in a bad relationship, if that sounds*
> *familiar at all ... I learned all about the fears*
> *of intimacy I had, the fears of being controlled,*
> *the fears of being smothered. The idea that I*
> *kind of have to take care of someone, then I*
> *resent them for a choice I made.*

It was still a long, painful road from there to his recov-ery, but Neil had at least gotten a handle on the aspects of his sex life that were so perplexing. **Call it one of the par-adoxes of masculinity: Sex, the thing that confuses and bothers us the most, is the one topic that we can only talk about in the form of jokes or one-upmanship.** In this way, the Sexual Mask is probably the most powerful one of the bunch. Its root is in our biology and our upbring-ing. We're wired for sex, and much of our childhood is spent navigating its terrain. For Neil, understanding all this was the end result of countless hours of therapy, emo-tional work, and trauma counseling. But many men don't do that work, and they wonder why they find themselves in predicaments that harm both them and their partners.

It's almost easy to chalk all of this up to biology. For a while, that's what I did. I would tell myself that monogamy was just a cultural invention or a tool the Church used to control people. Being with one woman for your whole life? That's not natural. Or, maybe it's cool for some guys, but those guys aren't as special or important or desirable as I am. After all, wouldn't an ancient man have to spread his DNA as far and wide as possible to make sure he passed on his genes? And wasn't that just a way of saying I could be with whomever I wanted, whenever I wanted, and that I was doing what my body was programmed to do?

The question is: How much of that script is cultural instead of biological? Think about the models of masculinity we have out there. Nearly all of them are connected to sex in some way. George Clooney—once named Sexiest Man Alive by *People* magazine—has held so much of that appeal for so long because he was the one man no woman could tie down. Movies and TV shows repeat this notion. Don Draper in *Mad Men* isn't just sexy because of his good looks; this character is sexy to people because he has a lot of sex. It isn't until the end of the show—when it's too late—that we (and he) learn how much he was using sex and infidelity to cover up his deep, deep psychological wounds. It wasn't until his life blew to pieces that he figured out that sex was a defense mechanism. I mean, Don Draper wasn't even his real name. His whole sexually charged identity was a literal mask!

And it isn't just fiction either. We perpetuate these stereotypes and myths in real life. Men who find and hook up with women are players, studs, ballers. Meanwhile, what's our take on a guy who is committed? He's

tied down. He's settled. He's off the market. He goes out with his buddies only when his wife gives him permission. He has a "dad bod." His sex life is a wasteland. And don't get me started with how unfair the labels and double standards are with women. What we celebrate in single guys, we call being a slut in a woman. When a guy marries a rich woman, it doesn't mean anything; but if a woman does it, she risks being called a gold digger. A woman who is clear about what she wants and expects in a relationship is a nag or a bitch.

It's all nonsense.

But this nonsense is rattling around in our heads when it comes to thinking about committed loving relationships. And it certainly doesn't make it easy for young impressionable men who are trying to figure out whom they should admire and emulate. All too often, they grow up thinking that single life equals fun and married life equals boredom.

It wasn't until I started opening up about my own issues that I began to think through all of this in any kind of systematic way. It took a lot of work and thought to figure out some of my issues, and that work isn't done.

Neil put it like this: "What happened was I realized the problem wasn't relationships. The problem was not her trying to control me. The problem wasn't monogamy. The problem was me . . . and the way I think." That resonated with me. I also was taking a problem I had and turning it into a problem that had been forced on me.

In my last book, *The School of Greatness*, I talked about being raped when I was 5 years old by a man who was our babysitter's son. It was a confusing experience, one that I didn't talk about for 25 years, that left me angry, frustrated, resentful, and defensive in many areas of my life. **An experience like that is hard to shake if you don't have the tools and emotional intelligence you need in order to heal, and what I later found is that the only way to heal a trauma like that is through sharing the story.**

However, when I was a freshman in college, I lived in a coed dorm and went through another challenging sexual experience. The dorm had bunk beds, and my roommate was a guy on the wrestling team. We always locked our door at night, but for whatever reason my roommate left in the middle of the night and the door stayed unlocked. I woke up at 3:00 a.m. with my pants down and a girl trying to have sex with me. I thought I was dreaming at first, as I was so exhausted from football practice the night before. Most guys might think this would be a dream come true, but for me it was a nightmare that was happening in real life.

I had met this girl a few times but didn't really know her. And even though I was a sexually turned-on man, I didn't want to have sex like this. The challenge was I had no strength at the time, and she was wrapping her arm around the bunk bed, pinning me down, trying to convince me and force sex on me. I told her to get off countless times and moved my head away when her drunken breath kept trying to kiss me, all while my pants were halfway down my legs, restricting me from moving. I finally woke up enough to get my legs up, and I literally kicked her off of me and onto the floor (don't worry, I wasn't on the top bunk). She tried to jump back on the bed, but like a kid with flailing legs kicking and screaming when they don't want to do something, I turned into Chuck Norris and started defending myself. She finally gave up and left my room. I had to get up 1 hour later for an early morning football weight room session, so I just shoved the whole experience away and got to practice.

Every woman is warned about these kinds of near-rape experiences, but not many men feel like this could happen to them. They have no vocabulary for talking to others about such experiences, and they fear if they did share them, they might get called something derogatory or be asked what's wrong with them.

One of the things I'm most grateful for in my life is my male friends and peers. They have been there for me, and they are willing to be straight up with me. My friend Tucker Max, for instance, is about as real as it gets. He too has struggled with relationships and monogamy. He's written books about his misadventures and gotten rich doing it. He used to have a website where women would email him to *ask* to have sex with him. He became a hero to a lot of guys for that reason. There was a time in my life when I would have seen that as "the life" too.

But that path took Tucker down a dark road. He might have had a great time, but he wasn't happy. At pivotal moments in his life—when he dealt with adversity or struggles—he felt alone. He had nothing in common with the women in his life. He didn't even know where to go to meet someone with whom he had anything in common. **When you have a toxic life, you attract only toxic people.** So he set out to change that from top to bottom. Now, he's written a serious book on how men can get their heads straight about issues like relationships and sexuality. And he was honest with me that it had taken him years of psychoanalysis to get his own head on straight about it all. But now that he has, he's a reservoir of insight and wisdom, especially about connection in relationships:

> *There are a lot of people, swingers and those types of guys, who say you can sleep with multiple women and have deep emotional connections with all of them. I don't believe that. Believe me, I have tested this. I wish it was true. I have lived with three women while I was sleeping with all of them . . .* I have never seen a situation where you're capable of having deep, intimate, trusting emotional connections with multiple women or with open relationships.

In other words, he was turning off a part of himself to make that "dream" possible. Or, in other cases, he was staying around people he didn't want to have a deeper connection with—it was the only way those superficial sexual relationships were possible.

Flash forward a few years. He's now happily married and has two children. The relationship he has built has been a source of strength and stability. He has a partner in the truest sense of that word. As he put it:

> *What I find in her . . . what I get out of this, is we have a deep emotional connection. I can trust her more than I've probably trusted anyone else in my life. I can be vulnerable with her. It's like having a soft place to land. I can confide in her. She's so supportive, she's so caring, she's so sweet. She's always on my side, not*

*literally but basically always on my side. She's
on my side.*

Coming from anyone else, those words might just
sound like empty platitudes, but we're talking about a guy
who has basically climbed every sexual peak possible. You
name it, he's done it. For him to use words like "trust" and
"connection" and "vulnerable" is saying something. And for
him to warn about the hazards of never-ending meaning-
less hookups is powerful, because it runs counter to almost
everything guys hear as they come of age in this culture:
Have sex or you're not a man. Then it progresses: Have a lot
of sex or you're not a man. Then it gets even worse: Start
having sex with only one woman . . . and you're less of a man.

These are scripts, not truths, but they operate as powerful cultural touchstones for a lot of guys. Masculinity and
sexuality become so tied up together that a lot of guys end
up confused and frustrated and feeling low or less than.
Add to that how difficult it is for parents to talk to their kids
about these things (especially dads, who themselves rarely
had a dad who did it well in their own childhood), and you
have a perfect recipe for disaster.

Thankfully, in no small part because of guys like Neil
and Tucker, we have finally started to explode some of
these myths (even if doing so has blown up in our faces on
occasion). **Here's a big-time myth that's taken root in
our culture: The more emotionally open and available
you are, the worse the sex gets. A lot of men reading
this right now are probably nodding their heads in
agreement. It turns out that the opposite is true: As a
whole bunch of recent research has proven, emotional**

intimacy increases both sexual desire and sexual libido.

When I asked Neil how his sex life has been after all the work he's done (and he agreed to answer the most personal of all personal questions!), he was refreshingly open and honest about it: "I thought that over time passion and sex fade in a relationship. It just gets old. But as we let go of our stories about each other and got closer emotionally, without fear, we keep having the best sex of our lives each time we have it."

When I first heard this, it hit me like a ton of bricks. Study after study shows this to be true—and when you think about it, it makes sense. **Truly great sex has at its root all the same stuff as emotional intimacy: being open with the other person about what you want; being able to communicate; being able to trust that the other person isn't going to think you're strange or crazy. Put more simply: Showing your emotions could lead to the best sex of your life.**

I'm not saying monogamy is right *for you,* or right for you *right now.* I'm not suggesting you try polyamory. I'm not saying you should dive right into a relationship or end the one you're in to go chase novelty. That's not what this is about. It's about how to remove the Sexual Mask, how to *think* about sex, and how to be aware about why you're making the decisions you're making about sex. Ultimately, it's about adding fulfillment to your life. Most men don't think about that, and I know this because for a long time, I didn't either. To some great degree, I know now that many of my issues in relationships were because I had just gone into so many of them mindlessly. I hadn't paid attention to the patterns; I hadn't done the kind of work that led me to ask, "What the hell am I doing with this girl?"

I think the process that men like Tucker and Neil and Chris have gone through to figure out how their sex life fits into their broader life is a valuable one. They have taken what is, for many men, a thoughtless thing that becomes a source of many issues and turned it into a way of thinking about all of their issues—familial, personal, relational, and emotional. **Stripping off the Sexual Mask, for them, revealed a great deal more than whether they prefer blondes or brunettes. It opened them up to who they were at their core, and it gave them the opportunities to have the richest relationships any of them have ever had.**

When I asked Tucker what he had learned after he had gotten married, he offered up a description that, I have to admit, sounded remarkable:

> Honestly, the thing that I've learned the most is how to be expressive and care and how to think about someone else's needs. *Someone who grew up in a normal family with brothers and sisters or was good at relationships will know that stuff intuitively. I don't know most of those things intuitively, so I've had to learn ... And Veronica [his wife] is pretty patient with me because she understands, "Okay, he doesn't get it."*

The best men I know have similar descriptions of their partnerships. And while I imagine that there are issues in their relationships, what I find is that they,

as a pair, work on them together. When the mask drops, in other words, something unique and powerful is revealed. I don't know if this is in the cards for everyone, but I imagine being in a fulfilling relationship is an ambition that most of us have—even if we have a limited idea of how to achieve it and an unlimited amount of fear about being vulnerable enough to admit it.

Toward the end of the book tour, my ex and I reconnected and got back together. Our relationship has been a great teacher for me. It's not perfect, and it probably never will be (that's true for any relationship). I'm not going to get everything I want all the time. She has her own needs, wants, and desires too. It seems like such an embarrassing discovery to learn that a woman in your life is a fully realized person too and is not just there to serve you per the role of "girlfriend," but it was a lesson I had to learn. I also learned how to be patient, and she's the one who has taught me patience. If I go back to the place of asking myself why I put up with even the slightest inconvenience or stress about relationships when there seem to be opportunities elsewhere, I remember that's just avoidance. What am I avoiding by not going deeper, by not having the tough conversations?

It strikes me that if a younger me had read what I just wrote, he would have been blown away. I might have even called me a pussy, or something like that. But that would have been the same avoidance talking, the same fear.

The process of getting underneath my Sexual Mask has made me face up to other things: my impatience, my (occasional) selfishness, and my issues. I had to struggle to think about the darker parts of my past, the ones that sometimes make my present more difficult than it should be. I had to struggle with what Neil called "the wounds underneath." I had to reckon with what I was avoiding.

So, what are you avoiding? What is your Sexual Mask hiding? Get at that stuff, and you might learn more about yourself than you ever have before.

| WHAT CAN WE DO RIGHT NOW? |

Sex is the perfect way to avoid emotions. It feels close and intimate, but sex allows a man struggling behind his Sexual Mask to compartmentalize those emotions and focus only on the physical aspects of sex. The problem with a singular focus on the physical part of sex is that it will never be enough. It's like a drug where you chase that first high until it drives you crazy, and so you move on to a new drug, and then another new drug, and then another new drug. A man trapped behind the Sexual Mask is always looking for the next good time and the next conquest, the newest, hottest one. And there's always someone newer and hotter. The cycle continues because sexual conquest is fundamentally an ego thing. Who you sleep with becomes who you are, and the number of women you've slept with determines your worth. It's not unlike the insatiable quest for riches that comes from wearing the Material Mask. It's a never-ending cycle.

What's Available When You Drop This Mask (Sexual)

Remember Sexual Man, you are a gift, and there's so much to celebrate about you. The people who care about you the most have been waiting to see what's behind your mask. It's time to reveal the real you. These are some of the things that can flood back into your life when you drop this mask.

Inner peace

Worthiness

Fulfilling intimate relationships

Feeling grounded

True partnership

MEN:

Figure out what you are avoiding. Is it responsibility? Self-worth? Intimacy, connection, pain, joy, or satisfaction? Are you dealing with a huge void or an overabundance of something you don't know how to handle? Make a list of those things you might be avoiding, and then create an action plan and the next steps you are committed to creating, and by when.

For example: I've been avoiding having a conversation with my girlfriend, and I'm going to call her tomorrow . . . whatever it is, write it down.

And really be honest with yourself about whether retreating behind this Sexual Mask has improved your life. **The key to figuring all this out is learning how to be alone. How to love yourself. You need to be in a relationship with yourself first. When you're looking for love and validation from the outside, you inevitably lose yourself and the ability to cultivate self-love because nothing inside you seems as valuable as what you get from someone else.** You'll never get enough from the outside to fill the void created on the inside, and so you must learn how to be happy by, and with, yourself.

One of the ways to do this is forgiveness. Sometimes the hardest person to forgive is yourself. Make a list of all the things in your life you still feel guilty for, and make a conscious decision to actually forgive yourself for each one of these items. At first it will be weird, but it will get easier over time as you learn to have this self-dialogue. I make mistakes all the time, but I always find time to forgive myself; otherwise, I'll always be hurting. The Sexual Mask is all about avoiding yourself . . . those feelings that you're not enough, and so you need someone else sexually to feel good because you can't get it from within.

Then write a letter to yourself describing all the things you love about you. This is only for you to see and experience.

WOMEN:

Find out what his vision is. Find out what matters to him. Find out what inspires him! This will support him in breaking through this mask. A man without a vision is a man who goes aimlessly through life. What makes him feel good in life, in work, in the world? What does he want from his friendships, his family relationships, his career, and his life? What are his dreams?

The more connected a man is to his vision, the more quickly that sexual void will be filled. Vision represents what a man wants, what he's committed to, and it's bigger than what his ego wants. When a man is trapped behind the Sexual Mask, his vision is blurry. Help him clear it up.

THE
AGGRESSIVE
MASK

In the meanest are all the
materials of manhood, only
they are not rightly disposed.

—HENRY DAVID THOREAU

IMAGINE THE MOMENTS just before a cage fight. The cheering crowd. The threatening opponent in the corner, flexing, shadow-boxing, bouncing rhythmically on the balls of his feet, ready for someone to ring the bell so he can pounce. The highlight reel of his past victories plays on the jumbotron—man after man hitting the canvas or tapping desperately as the air gets choked out of them. Think about all the money on the line. The bragging rights. The years of training that led up to this moment.

And now think, how would you feel if you were the fighter about to enter the cage to face your opponent? Afraid? Anxious? Angry? Numb? Worried? You'd be a perfectly normal human being to feel those things.

And yet, if you listen to Andy Cona, a British cage fighter, describe this moment, he doesn't feel anything of the sort. Here's his mind right before he is about to step into the ring: "From the second I walk through them doors to the second I walk out . . . all [my] problems go away. The second you walk out the door . . . your problems are back."

In other words, *your* problem might be stepping into the ring in the first place; but for Andy, the ring is the place *his* problems are kept at bay. He goes on:

> *The first fight I ever had was like a release. Like, "I'm allowed to hit this lad, and it's making me feel better." See, I don't have a family. Me and my brother were put into [foster] homes. He was everything—he was my mom, my dad, my brother, and my sister. He was everyone, and then he killed himself. I've never, ever told anyone that. I don't like to show people weakness. I'm broken inside, I know I am.*

There is something admirable about the degree to which Andy knows that his issues are what drive his fighting. That he's even willing to admit them suggests that maybe he's not broken; he's just bruised. He's fixable. **But still, there's something scary about taking years of childhood issues and pain and channeling them outward at a total stranger for money and fame. As Andy's**

story reveals, for the most part, the pain you inflict on others never reduces the pain you are trying to escape from within yourself.

No one understands that better than two-time Super Bowl champion, seven-time first team All-Pro, and 13-time Pro Bowl linebacker Ray Lewis. Lewis's intensity and aggressiveness are legendary. He played the game at one speed: full. He spent 17 seasons with the Baltimore Ravens terrorizing NFL quarterbacks, running backs, and tight ends. It was a fitting profession for a man who spent the first 17 years of his life terrorized by hate and anger toward an absent father. When I sat down to talk with him about life, success, struggle, and manhood, the benefit of hindsight and reflection as a 41-year-old man allowed him to really crystallize how his upbringing impacted his life:

> There are certain moments in a child's life that a father should never miss because when you replace [that influence], most of the time you replace it with things that get you in trouble. *I replaced it with dominance over another individual. I had hate for my father, and that hate turned into fuel. I don't encourage anybody to live the way I lived.*

That probably seems like an odd warning from a man who turned all that aggression into tens of millions of dollars, but what you're forgetting is that it was only beneficial in one place: the gridiron. Everywhere else, it had no place.

This is a somewhat modern phenomenon, since for tens

of thousands of years, acts of aggression and physical dominance have been how men have ordered themselves within families, tribes, and societies. It would be foolish to deny that aggression has played, and continues to play, a huge part in male development.

Ask any schoolteacher, parent, or coach about their experiences managing and mentoring young boys, and invariably you'll hear stories about crazy roughhousing, endless competitions, and yes, fighting. All of this, in many ways, is accepted *and expected* behavior: Boys will be boys, the old saying goes.

The thing is, modern society has evolved to such a point that aggression and physical dominance are no longer the only—or even the preeminent—means by which men can order themselves. By and large, violence and aggression have disappeared from the daily existence of most people in most developed nations. So when we see it in our sons, in fighters, and in athletes like Andy and Ray, it feels abnormal, even though it isn't.

That said, the real problem for the development of young men is when aggression is the primary outlet for their pain, their sadness, their anxiety, and their anger.

Unaddressed anger is the glue that keeps the Aggressive Mask stuck in place, starting very early and lasting, in many cases, for decades. There is research on this, and it testifies to how much young boys, in particular, are soaked in anger. For many of them, anger is the only emotion that is "acceptable" to express. But for too many boys, that anger is just a cover—a gloss on the hard realities of their lives. Harvard Medical School professor W. S. Pollack, in a research paper about adolescent rites of passage, puts it like this:

*Behind their masks of pseudoinvulnerability
and the drama of action, the one full emotion
boys are "allowed" to express within the nar-
row bandwidth of developing masculinity—*
Anger—*it is often hard to hear boys' stifled but
genuine voices of pain and struggle, their
yearning for reconnection.*[1]

If you think about it for even a minute, this starts to
make sense. Anger is a shield. It protects us and helps us
respond to moments when we feel small, helpless, and
weak. That was certainly the case for both Andy Cona and
Ray Lewis.

It doesn't take long for cultural influences of violence
to begin to creep into boys' lives. And soon enough boys are
using those very influences to vent their simmering anger.
Take video games, for example. I'm not talking about the
violence—even though it's pervasive. I'm more interested in
how anger dominates these games. As Ashly Burch, a writer
and actor, told me:

*When an emotion sneaks in for a male charac-
ter [in video games], by and large, it is anger.
And any sort of grief is very, very underplayed
and never actually discussed or processed.
Kids end up really looking up to this character.
And what they end up idolizing is someone who
cannot express themselves emotionally, cannot be honest or open with anyone around
them.*

So is it any wonder then that young boys, awash in
anger and fed a diet of virtual violence, end up fighting with

each other? Is it any wonder that those same boys end up as grown men with anger and violence problems? Is this how our society perpetuates a climate where aggression is the most acceptable emotional outlet for men? Every time we see a male celebrity get into a fistfight over some perceived slight; every time some pro player beats up his wife or girlfriend; every time we see a fresh case of violent aggression in the media—we're all left sort of scratching our heads. Recall that violence is now a daily norm for most of us. Should we be so puzzled? **The very things that little boys do to each other to flush that toxic, inexplicable (to them) anger, fear, and sadness out of their systems cause huge social and personal problems when those little boys turn into big men who have not dealt with their underlying pain.** Sometimes these patterns are reinforced in the home, and this compounds the problem. When Andy, the emotionally broken cage fighter, talks about taking all of that pain and rage and hurt and bringing it into the ring, you could credit him, at least, with finding an outlet that isn't going to violate the law.

But this aggression, this male need for combat, is a mask—and it's something that we need to think about and explore further. It's something that, at least for me, has been hardwired into my body for a long time. When I grew up, I got into the usual scuffles that boys do, but I also got into some very scary, violent fights that weren't driven by rivalry, but rather were motivated by the fear of vulnerability and then rage.

In *The School of Greatness,* I told the story of the time when I was 12 years old raking grass with a couple other kids. Our roughhousing and goofing around turned into a fight when two of us ganged up on the other kid without realizing that was what we were doing. Feeling victimized, he sucker punched me in the back of the head. That sent me into a blind rage that resulted in me pummeling him until you could barely recognize him by looking at him. My reaction, I understand now, was born out of being victimized myself as a boy and not having the tools to deal with the pain and the shame. Aggression and anger were the only tools in my emotional tool kit.

A couple years later, I entered high school and found football. Because I was big and athletic, I could be good at it, but also, if I'm being honest, it allowed me to smash guys to the ground and be rewarded for this behavior. Football didn't just allow it, it encouraged it. Contact sports were an outlet for all that anger I'd kept inside for so long. I relished the feeling: It started in my head, the anger bubbling and boiling, and then it transferred to my legs, which took off, and then my whole body would smash whatever and whoever was in my way. And when I did that, I felt exactly the kind of release that Andy described. For a few minutes or hours, I wasn't mad at being picked last, I wasn't mad about people calling me dumb, I wasn't mad about my family stresses or parents arguing, and I wasn't mad about being raped as a young boy. For a little while, I wasn't mad at all. It was great for me—though it probably wasn't great for the unfortunate soul whom I just leveled on the football field.

That's good, right? Better some guy ends up on the ground in a game than in real life? Well, the answer is: sort of. I know now that I was transferring rage from other parts of my life into sports. **The difficulties in my family, the sexual abuse I suffered, the feelings of instability and**

inadequacy, the normal struggle of being a kid who was picked last and picked on—all of it came out in ways that were physical and brutal. And even though I vented my rage on the playing field, it didn't mean that the roots of that anger weren't equally dangerous. I was a kid, and I had no idea what to do with all of that rage. I had two options: I could leave all those painful feelings bottled up inside, or, just like Ray Lewis described, I could use them as fuel to punish other people. I chose the latter, in the form of sports. So do many young boys. So do many adult men.

There's a quote I think about a lot: "Violence is nurturance turned backward." It's from Nora Samaran, who wrote a powerful essay about rape culture and the need to nurture males. It's no surprise to me that this essay went viral. Here's what she's getting at: **If you think about it, men who come of age without being nurtured and without learning how to nurture themselves have a hole they carry around. Some people fill this hole with drugs or alcohol; others fill it with violence. But it gets filled, one way or another.**

I'm not here to criticize sports. I have been blessed with the opportunities I've had because of sports. I've had amazing coaches, incredible experiences, and teammates whom I consider family. But I also endured a lot of hardship and injury and suffering. I also did a lot of things that I regret, and I hurt myself in ways that I'm still paying the price for. Above all, I was left with an important set of questions: Was it really healthy? Was that the best way to live? What kind of damage was I doing to my body, mind, and heart in the process? I didn't take the time to answer those questions when I was playing, but in hindsight, I know the answers aren't pretty. I was often using sports as a way of refusing to deal with the big anger issues I had, and my guess is that I wasn't the only one.

I don't mean to make anger out to be something all bad. There are times and moments when anger, properly harnessed, is necessary and can even be an effective tool. **But the use of anger and aggression can also corrode the person expressing it. For some men, like myself, this well of anger is something we have to keep a close eye on. If we let it, this anger can steadily take over our lives in ways that are destructive, or it can surprise us out of nowhere and potentially derail everything we've been working toward.**

What does someone who has a handle on this violence inside them look like? Well, they look like Randy Couture, the MMA fighter. During our epic conversation (I still think about that interview), he told me a little bit about how he got his start in fighting. It had to do with the breakdown of his family, specifically his dad leaving when he was little:

> If I wasn't good enough for my own dad to be around, there was always that kind of doubt in the back of my mind that I had to prove myself, I had to earn it somehow. *That's why I got into the sport of wrestling. I knew, through stories from my mom, that he was a wrestler. He wrestled, so I thought maybe I'd get his attention if I wrestled, and it didn't work out that way, but I found where I was supposed to be. I found the thing I was good at. I found the thing that*

*helped me travel down the road and gain that
appreciation and value in myself.*

Randy's story is virtually the spitting image of Ray Lewis's story. Ray was a champion wrestler in Florida when he was in high school, just like his dad. One day during his sophomore year, his wrestling coach was driving him home from school—something he did every day, having taken on a father figure role in Ray's life—and he asked Ray what drove him. Uncharacteristically, Ray was brutally vulnerable and honest: "I just don't know why my father don't come see me." It was like, maybe if Ray was truly great at the same thing his dad was great at, it might change something.

Of course, that's never how it works. A boy's ability in athletics is never why men leave their families, and it is rarely what it takes to bring them back. This truth is something that is very hard for boys, especially, to understand because so many of them have been raised in a culture where their value is defined by their performance in competition. **Being great is supposed to mean that they are good boys, which should mean that they are good enough sons to be worthy of their fathers' attention. When that doesn't happen, boys typically turn the resulting pain into anger, and that anger into violence.**

What's so surprising and exceptional about Randy Couture is that none of the stuff he brought into the ring spilled out into his life . . . ever. For Andy and Ray, the ring or the mat was an outlet very early on, but it wasn't a cage— it didn't trap all the aggression inside, at least not initially. Randy was different somehow. He never got into trouble with that stuff in school. "I was never a fighter. I never got into fights ... I had maybe two street fights all through school, and maybe that was because I was on the mat getting all that physical-ness out," he told me. The pain he brought to the mat stayed on the mat. He was processing his anger too; he was learning discipline and character and the other important things that sports teach. He wasn't just looking for targets and scapegoats.

It showed in his demeanor as an adult, as well. Randy was as tough a fighter as they came, but he didn't walk into the ring with a chip on his shoulder. As he put it, "Even walking out, walking out the tunnel, walking out to the cage, I was always winking, smiling, you know. This is what I'm here for; this is what I trained to do. I'm here to have a good time and show everybody what I've been working on, and this is my opportunity. It wasn't about anger or animosity, aggression, any of those things. There's a difference between being competitive and *being*."

I think of Randy and Ray as the kind of examples all young kids should learn from. Randy made choices you should learn to follow from the very beginning; Ray made choices you should learn to avoid from the beginning. Together they make up the right kind of coach. They're two sides of the same coin. Neither is some angry man teaching boys to be angry men. For Randy, the sports of wrestling and MMA were ways to learn diligence, to learn how to practice, and to achieve excellence. For Ray, wrestling and football were ways to exorcise emotional demons and to work his way out of a bad situation. They had rough childhoods, and, sure, getting some of that out on the mat was useful to them. But eventually—one sooner than the other—they didn't feel the need to fight angry. They weren't fighting or hitting full speed because they were perpetually pissed. For them, the fighting and the hitting became an exercise in defining character. Randy put it this way:

> *The sport of wrestling is one of those few sports,*
> *I think, that develop that kind of character.*
> *You spend the time, run the extra mile, do the*
> *extra drilling, you know it's gonna pay off and*
> *you're gonna see the results and you're gonna*
> *win the matches, the close matches, the tough*
> *matches, and I think that I learned that from*
> *the sport and from those guys that taught me*
> *and made me work in the sport.*

Sports were something similar for me. As I matured, and as the anger dissipated a bit for me, I found in sports the kind of discipline and depth that I was looking for. It gave me goals, motivation, teammates, and training. I had my share of hard, angry moments, but I also found the same kind of joy in sports that Randy describes.

One of the more revealing moments in all of Randy's training came when he was practicing Greco-Roman wrestling. He talks about how he saw grown men tear up because of the pain and suffering. It wasn't surprising, in a way, because the matches were so brutal. About the training, he said, "You're gonna wrestle for the next 90 minutes straight. Nowhere to hide, nowhere to go. And that's the first time I've seen grown men actually break down and cry." I pressed him on this a bit. Wouldn't crying in that kind of masculine environment be the opposite of what you'd expect? Wouldn't the other guys give you all kinds of hell for it? "No, it was never like that. You were never gonna chastise that guy because that could be you tomorrow. You don't know," he said. The crying didn't take anything away from how brutal the environment was. There's an old line from the ancients: "He is best who is trained in the severest school." That's what training in that environment was like, so a few tears were forgiven.

Randy's story—from sports to self-discipline and then achievement—is, in some ways, what we'd want for our young men. **It isn't enough to simply hope that boys and men give up the aggression that lives within them; it might be more accurate, though, to want them to channel it, learn about it, study it, understand it, and also drop it when appropriate.** As Randy put it, "I started it for the wrong reasons, probably to get my dad's attention, but I found what I loved, I found what I wanted to do, so it worked out."

Randy's words reminded me a lot of how Steve Cook, the bodybuilder, talked about his focus on athletics. This is also a good reminder to all of us about how these masks so often overlap and reinforce each other. You don't have to look very far to find examples of a world full of men who are trapped behind both the Athlete Mask and the Aggressive Mask. Randy could have very easily found himself in that position. To the extent that he has lived a life free from those masks while finding an outlet for the anger inside him, which also made him a better man, Randy is one of the lucky ones.

I shudder to think what someone capable of his kind of violence might have done if he hadn't found that outlet.

What does that look like? Well, look around. Look at kids who bully other kids. Look at kids who shoot up their schools or join street gangs, or kids who resort to any sort of nonstructured, noncompetitive violence. Kids take drugs or direct their anger inward until they feel they don't deserve to live anymore (and then commit an act of *self*-violence). Each of these kids probably has a kernel of what Randy had inside him, but the combination of that and their circumstances has turned them poisonous.

I'm not the biggest fan of ascribing everything about who we are to some childhood incident. It's important to know that we can change, and that we're not who we are at 5 years old forever. But the truth is, childhood is also when we begin to get a real sense of self. We start to figure out what matters to us and what doesn't; what bothers us and what doesn't; and how the world is shaped around us. So when we think about adult men who get into fistfights at bars, it isn't too much of a stretch to imagine that their childhoods carried the seeds of some of that anger.

This can sound a bit woo-woo, but Nora Samaran's point about what happens when we turn nurturance backward is one worth taking seriously. She writes, **"Compassion for self and compassion for others grow together and are connected; this means that men finding and recuperating the lost parts of themselves will heal everyone."**[2] It's tough not to buy the argument that being able to love others and being able to love yourself are two sides of the same coin, and that many men grow up being able to do neither. There are countless causes for that, and this book isn't the place for that complete diagnosis. But what we can do is think about how those feelings end up calcifying into a mask of anger and aggression that men carry around.

And what's behind that mask? A whole bunch of weakness, fear, and feelings of unworthiness. Here's one of the more interesting ways I've seen this put, by Professor Pollack:

> Women are emotionally educated in understanding and expressing a wider range of emotions than men. Socially, it is more acceptable for women to express sadness, fear, disappointment, or embarrassment. In contrast, a myriad of men are emotionally uneducated, not having learned how to constructively express negative emotions, such as fear, embarrassment, or guilt. As a result, they may cover these primary negative emotions with secondary negative emotions, such as anger.[3]

I think that phrase "emotionally uneducated" is important because it defines a problem we can fix. We can do something. For men, it means we can begin that education; for people who take care of boys, it means we can be attuned to the emotions that boys may not have yet developed and that we want them to cultivate.

Here's the thing: This struggle is made all the more difficult because, as a society, there is a huge amount of confusion about boys, aggression, testosterone, and violence. When people say "Well, boys will be boys," they tend to assume that, as a matter of course, boys are just going to be violent and hurt people. If pressed, those same people will say, "Well, it's testosterone. It makes boys and men act the way they do." Not only is this a cheap excuse, it's also wrong. Much good research is beginning to challenge our view of this. For instance, Professor C. A. Robarcheck, writing about the culture of the Semoi in Malaysia, has found evidence challenging these claims. "While popular belief unflinchingly claims that testosterone is the source for male aggression," he writes, "the Semoi of Malaysia has both men and women co-create one of the most peaceful societies in the world. Aggression is not praised in men in that culture. From a young age, children are taught non-violence, since these Malaysians believe that aggression increases the likelihood of illness and disaster."

He goes on:

> *Testosterone's reputation, however, goes far beyond any grounding in scientific literature.* A recent review of scientific studies of preadolescent and early adolescent boys concludes that the research literature "provides no evidence of an association between testosterone and aggressive behavior." *One example, a study done at the Bronx Children's Psychiatric Center in New York, measured the testosterone levels of the center's most violent young boys. The researchers found that none of the boys had blood levels of testosterone that were outside the normal range or were significantly different from those of a group of nonaggressive children of the same age and race to whom they were being compared.*[4]

In other words, even the most brutal kids in a psychiatric center had no more testosterone floating around in their bloodstreams than usual. This is all a long way of saying that chalking up this kind of aggression to a chemical cause is a way of getting out of having tough conversations about the kinds of boys and men we're producing.

Let's go back to the Semoi for a minute. They have a society that they've made this way; they haven't just accepted violence as the way of the world. And they aren't the only ones, either: "Within North America, culturally distinct groups such as the Hutterian Brethren, the largest and most successful Christian communal group in the United States, or the Amish, have been astonishingly peaceful, perhaps more so than any other of the peaceful societies known to anthropology. For over 350 years no Hutterite living within his own community has slain another community member," writes Robarcheck.

The point here isn't to imagine that we can, in a minute, remake the world in the image of the Semois or Hutterites. No, the point is to question the amount of aggression we have in our society—and in ourselves—and whether or not we can do something to mediate it. Robarcheck's conclusion is both infuriating and inspiring: **"A destiny of aggression isn't born, it's made, most notably in societies like ours in which aggressive impulses are allowed free rein. We can raise boys to be nonviolent if we so choose."**[5]

And this idea—that we can raise boys to be nonviolent—is something worth taking seriously, given the facts. Think of one of the great problems of our time: mass shootings.

According to Lin Huff-Corzine, a sociologist, "Between 2001 and 2010, less than 8 percent of mass murder offenders in the US were women, based on data from the FBI. Not to mention, some of the women included in the statistics assisted in a crime but did not pull a trigger themselves."[6]

The journalist James Hamblin, writing in *The Atlantic,* has come to a simple conclusion about these mass killings: "Masculinity [is] a more common feature [in mass shootings] than any of the elements that tend to dominate discourse—religion, race, nationality, political affiliation, or any history of mental illness."[7]

Is it crazy to think that behind a lot of these killings is a history of weakness and fear and pain and abuse? No. What's crazy, I think, is imagining that those who suffer in that way *won't* act out in a violent or aggressive manner. What's crazy is thinking that boys who walk around with a hole inside them *won't* find a way to fill it either with negative, self-destructive things or with behaviors that ultimately project the pain out onto others.

And this isn't just about male-on-male violence either. Domestic abuse expert Lundy Bancroft identifies a man's "values and beliefs" that lead to domestic abuse. Things that shape those include role models, media, and religions. **The research shows that the embrace of traditional masculinity increases the possibility of domestic violence and abuse committed by a man. If you're told all your life to "man up," and you're not taught any of the other things a man ought to do, then is it any wonder that you'd grow up thinking that a fist is the solution to everything? If you're told that your physical domi-**

nance over a woman is what makes you a man, how else would you act?

One of the great things I have learned over the course of my efforts at personal growth and self-improvement is that giving up some of your anger allows you to walk around the world with a bit more lightness. This doesn't mean you can't protect yourself when you need to; it's just that you start to turn down the volume on those moments when you are most aggressive. Think of it like losing weight—you feel quicker and more agile on the balls of your feet because that excess poundage isn't slowing you down.

In the middle of my conversation with Ray Lewis, I asked him about his definition of a man and whether it had evolved as he got older, had kids, became successful, and ultimately retired. By way of answering my question, he told me a story about when he came to a deeper understanding of the challenges the men in his family have faced.

He was 33 years old. He'd reengaged with his long-absent father, and his father wanted him to meet a man named Shady Ray Whitehead who lived in some little trailer 6 hours outside of Charlotte, North Carolina. He had no idea where they were going or who this man was they were visiting, but when they arrived, he and his father walked in and his father said, "Meet your grandfather."

Ray sat on the floor while his dad sat on the couch, and they talked. One of the first things out of his father's mouth was a question to his grandfather that had also run through Ray's head nearly every day of the first 17 years of his life: "Dad, why'd you leave me?" To say this blindsided Ray would be an understatement.

Ray sat with this information for a while, listening to

his father and grandfather, and started to think about the men in his family who struggled in their relationships. Ray's realization is something out of a novel, or a sermon:

> *This is a generational curse, man. My son is 21, I'm 41, my father is 61, my grandfather's 81. His father is 101. Five generations. Twenty years apart. What are we doing? I rode back home with my father for 6 hours while he kept talking, and I never said a word. When I got done listening to him, I said to him:* "You know what a man is? A man accepts all of the wrongs, never complains, forgives, and then moves on." *That's what a man does, because you can never replace him not being to a football game. Never replace him not being to a wrestling match, or a track meet. Beat up by a group of kids? You can never replace him not being there. You can never replace that. So what you can replace is you can replace it with moving on.*

This is our work to do. The rewards are, indeed, waiting for us, but they will not make themselves known until we begin the process of dropping our Aggressive Mask.

| WHAT CAN WE DO RIGHT NOW? |

A man who struggles with aggression needs, first and foremost, to channel his energy and anger in a constructive direction. There are a number of ways to do this at a practical level:

- Create a wrecking room in your house where you can get it out safely. Fill it with things to smash, push, hit, and pummel. If you can't get a room, get a pillow. Beat the hell out of it. And repeat.
- Do cathartic shouting exercises once a week. Scream it out!
- Take a boxing class, work out, swim, or run.
- Create an affirmation (e.g., "I'm a peaceful, joyful, loving man") that you say when you want to break something or get aggressive.

These are things that can support you in the moment, but at a fundamental level, you need to go deeper than that. You need to figure out what's really bothering you so you can let go of it.

What's Available When You Drop This Mask (Aggressive)

Remember Aggressive Man, you are a gift, and there's so much to celebrate about you. The people who care about you the most have been waiting to see what's behind your mask. It's time to reveal the real you. These are some of the things that can flood back into your life when you drop this mask.

Inner peace

Emotional control

Responsiveness versus reactiveness

Self-awareness

Forgiveness of others and yourself

Patience

True strength

MEN:

Make a list of the people who hurt you. Who beat you, ignored you, abandoned you, yelled at you, degraded you, or rejected you? Write out exactly who they were, what they did to you, and how it made you feel. Let it live on the page instead of on a loop in your head. Then, hardest of all, you need to start the process that Ray Lewis highlighted in his story. You need to own what happened, forgive the people who hurt you, and move on.

WOMEN:

Share your experiences of being hurt by aggressive people and how it affected you. Describe what happened and how they made you feel and what you wanted to do about it. Let the men in your life who are struggling know that there is life after this pain and that the emotions it brings to the surface are difficult to accept but possible to deal with. We can turn pain into purpose if we make a conscious effort to do so.

THE JOKER MASK

Humor can be used as a mask
that shields both the wearer
and those around him, from
the pain underneath.

—MIKHAIL LYUBANSKY

I'VE INTERVIEWED A lot of people for my podcast, and I've
come to expect that I will be asked some version of this
question: *If you could sit down with anyone, dead or alive,
and ask them any question, who would it be?* I can think of a
few names, and high on that list would be Robin Williams.

There's a lot I'd like to ask him. I'd like to ask him how
someone can do so much in one lifetime. How can you win
Oscars, Emmys, *and* Grammys? How do you go from a life

in stand-up comedy to a life on the silver screen? How do you do movies that are hilariously funny and then switch it up and do dramas that stir the heart? What was it like making *Mrs. Doubtfire*? I'd ask. How did you go from being this shy, quiet kid to becoming an international sensation, someone who changed the game of comedy forever?

But then the conversation would have to turn serious. I'd want to ask him about his masks, his pain, the difficulties he faced in achieving as much as he did. If he's like most of my guests, he'll have his share of those. But then, he'd probably have a bit more, given the scale of his success and the stages on which he lived his life. And my guess is that no matter how hard I tried to pry, I wouldn't be able to make much progress. Robin Williams was a professional, and I bet he'd be able to answer without letting the Joker Mask slip even a little bit.

I don't remember where I was when I heard the news in the fall of 2014 that Robin Williams had committed suicide. The world's heart was heavy. So was mine. Even President Obama had this to say: "He was one of a kind. He arrived in our lives as an alien—but he ended up touching every element of the human spirit." Remembrances poured in from around the world. His daughter said that the "world is forever a little darker, less colorful, and less full of laughter in his absence"—and she was right.

The whole tragic end calls to mind a point that writer Zara Barrie made in an essay she wrote exploring the connection between darkness and humor: **"The effects of making another person laugh are reminiscent of a fast-acting drug; you feel instantly better—and the results are addictive. Sad people make careers out of making us laugh."**[1]

For the better part of his career, Robin Williams struggled with addictions to cocaine and alcohol. When a close friend died of an overdose, Williams briefly cleaned up his act. He took to cycling, something that he says saved his life. But it was a solitary pursuit, a kind of symbol that revealed he wanted to be on his own, on a bike, pedaling away. I didn't know Robin Williams, and even though I know people like him, I can't begin to imagine the pain he must have been going through when he took his own life. I imagine that most of those around him were so shocked when it happened: He may not have shared the parts of himself that were most deeply in pain and most in need of help. He preferred instead to focus on others and take away their pain by doing what he did best: playing the part of the joker, the part that had made his life what it was.

In the wake of his death, every news show, talk show, and interview show spent at least half of one episode remembering and eulogizing Robin Williams. Maybe they asked their previously scheduled guest if they had any Robin stories, or they'd invite on someone who they knew was an old, great friend—people like Bobcat Goldthwait or Billy Crystal—to share some insight and help audiences make sense of the tragedy. In nearly every case it seemed, no matter who it was, they had a story about a time on the set of a film or backstage after a comedy show when Robin had everyone in stitches, breaking whatever tension or anger may have been present, by riffing on the entire room, sometimes for 20 or 30 minutes, until people were dying with laughter instead of crying with frustration.

On the set of *Schindler's List*, he'd call Steven Spielberg to lighten the mood and lift his spirit as the heaviness of that true story started to take its toll on the director.

After his friend Christopher Reeve (aka Superman) was

paralyzed in a horse-riding accident, Robin snuck into his hospital room the day before Reeve's first corrective surgery, disguised as a doctor with a Russian accent, and announced that he was ready to proceed with Reeve's rectal examination! Robin regularly spent time at St. Jude Children's Hospital, entertaining the kids and the staff for as long as it took to make everyone laugh.

But it's the story that Minnie Driver tells about the famous park scene in *Good Will Hunting* that sticks out to me. In the scene, Robin and Matt Damon are seated on a bench in Boston Common. Ironically enough, the scene starts with young Will Hunting cracking jokes about the quiet serenity of their location, clearly uncomfortable with this intimate moment. The jokes set the opening tone of the scene and make up pretty much all of Matt Damon's lines. The rest belong to Robin Williams, in a 4-minute speech about love and loss and vulnerability that is sad, moving, heartbreaking, and insightful all at the same time. It's the scene that won him the Oscar for best supporting actor that year.

We know now that the speech probably spoke to a lot of the issues Robin struggled with over his life, but what Minnie Driver—their costar and fellow Oscar nominee—remembers is that around lunchtime, as people came to the park to eat, word spread around that Robin Williams was down in the Common filming a movie. "He did this amazing impromptu stand-up routine to all the people eating their sandwiches on the Common, and people were coming out of buildings because they heard he was doing this," Driver told an interviewer back in 2014. "At the end of lunch, there were about 300 people. He was a good man."[2]

To me, Robin Williams epitomizes a man who wears the Joker Mask. And stories like the one Minnie Driver tells reveal the essence of such a man who tries to deflect pain—his or others'—with humor or sarcasm. Not many people want to feel the pain they feel or connect with the trauma they're facing in their lives, be it relationships, death, insecurity, losing a job, or not feeling worthy of love. It's hard for people to look at that and be okay with themselves—so they deflect. **Men who wear this mask deflect this pain with humor so they never have to feel it. The opposite of pain is pleasure, or joy, and that's the thing they want to focus on the most—the thing they don't have.**

Many people do this, of course. Most guys do this at one time or another. It's a pretty effective defensive mechanism, for a while. But when it becomes pervasive and dominant, then it is more than a mechanism—it's a mask. In Robin Williams's case, you could argue that with his growing depression, it's a mask that extended his life for several years. I would never fault him for that. I would never judge him or question his choices. You do what you have to do to survive; it's just a shame that we are so bad at equipping the men in our culture with the tools they need to deal with this pain in the first place.

I've put up my fair share of fronts in my life. I have a long history of focusing on fun over pain. As a kid, I was always trying to be the fun, goofy guy who was outrageous in photos, anything to bring light to the moment. One reason I did this was because I didn't think I could contribute intelligence, so instead I brought humor, especially around my family. Even now, when things aren't going great and someone asks me how things are, my instinctive response is, "Good, but tell me how *you're* doing?" **Like many people, I want to avoid being the dark cloud in other people's lives, so I pretend things are sunny, even when**

**they are obviously not. So I keep things light, or at sur-
face level. I want to talk about other people. I want to
focus on other people's challenges because focusing on
my own feels more vulnerable.**

One of the most popular comedic personalities online
currently (with more than 100 million views of his hilarious satirical videos) is my spirit animal JP Sears. You probably would recognize his long red hair and flower headband.
In my interview with him, between cracking jokes, we got
serious about why he learned to use humor. He told me:

> My sense of humor developed because it helped
> me compensate for my pain. If I felt insignifi-
> cant inside, which I did during my childhood, I
> learned if I can make someone laugh, it feels
> like they value me. And if they value me, then it
> means I'm significant. *And if I'm significant
> because I just made them laugh, then I don't feel
> the sense of insignificance that I'm relentlessly
> trying to escape from. I became addicted to
> making people laugh. It was my survival strat-
> egy. The good thing about that was it helped
> train me to become a black belt of comedy.*

**Beneath the jokes is often a sadness or some
problem. Behind the mask—no matter how funny or
entertaining—is a real person.** Psychologist Edward
Dreyfus puts it even more directly: "Perhaps we should listen more attentively to those who hide behind the mask of
humor. Perhaps we should be asking them to whom do they
turn to make them laugh? Perhaps we should spend a little

more effort in seeing the person behind the mask." If we had listened to what Robin Williams was saying behind his mask, I wonder what we would have heard.

I can relate here. I spent my entire educational years doing anything to avoid my fear of being made to feel stupid. I would constantly pull my best friend, Matt (who had a full-ride academic scholarship and a 4.0 GPA before he met me), away from his studies in college to goof off and go out to have fun. Anything to distract me from doing the important thing that I dreaded—studying. When his GPA dropped below the minimum requirement to keep his scholarship, and he had to start paying for tuition for the first time ever, I didn't even feel bad. I could see how much more fun he was having and that I was bringing joy to his life. By the way, he's still one of my best friends 12 years later, so apparently I'm forgiven.

The essay I mentioned earlier by Zara Barrie is an extended meditation on this topic. She wonders why so many of the funniest people she knows are also some of the darkest. She takes a guess:

> *So many comedians/funny people will tell you they grew up feeling hopelessly inadequate, hideously ugly, impossibly fat, meekly small, and direly insignificant.* These deep-rooted insecurities are what provided them with a die-hard desire and unrelenting ambition to be seen, respected, and accepted by their peers. Society will accept you for your flaws, so long as you're funny. *Taking on the role as the class clown at school is the ultimate way for the incessantly bullied kid to gain popularity.*[3]

Humor becomes the ultimate mask—one that gets you what you've always wanted (acceptance) for being the opposite of who you've always been (different). Not surprisingly, this detachment from the emotions and the identity hidden behind the mask can have profound effects on relationships, on professional life, and on overall happiness. The Joker Mask can also prevent you from finding answers to questions that have tormented you all your life, because you lack the tools to be serious for long enough to ask them directly.

In 2016, a stand-up comedian from New England named Ray Harrington released a documentary called *Be a Man*. Ray is a mountain of a dude. He's 6 feet 7 inches tall and probably weighs more than 300 pounds. If he were into football, he'd have the ideal size for a left tackle. The premise of the documentary is that Ray, who was raised without a father in his life, is about to have his first child—a boy—and he wants to learn all the stuff about being a man that he never got to learn from his absent father, so he can teach them to *his* son and be the dad he never had.

It's a great idea and a very touching sentiment, but in the documentary it seemed like Ray could never get out from behind his Joker Mask. Everything was a joke. The areas of traditional manhood that he focused on were fighting, driving, drinking, shaving, and dressing. He got in the ring with a champion boxer despite never having been in a fight. He drove a Ferrari, then went to visit the largest private collection of *Back to the Future* memorabilia, including the DeLorean. He went to a bar and got drunk trying to find "his drink," because a man is supposed to know what his drink is. He went and got a hot shave with a straight razor, then tried to shave with one himself at home. He had a wardrobe makeover and then stood in front of a panel of women to be judged on how manly he was.

If you're like most people who read this description, you're probably chuckling to yourself because it sounds kind of funny. And I guess that's the point. Ray *is* a comedian after all. But when the credits rolled at the end of the documentary, as Ray delivered a monologue in voice-over about how being a man is about being comfortable with who you are, I wondered if Ray actually believed his own words. I wondered if Ray really got to ask the questions that have nagged at him since he was a boy, growing up without a dad. And I wonder if he got the answers he needed. Because it felt like he was pulling from the clichés and punchlines of popular culture's idea of what manhood is and then, at the end, what our culture tells us he's *supposed* to think nowadays as an evolved modern man.

There was a really good idea in this documentary, but it felt like it was never fully realized because the professional joker who made it didn't know how to fully remove the Joker Mask, whose very existence was probably the reason why this documentary seemed like a good idea to him in the first place.

Don't get me wrong, there are a lot of good things to take from *Be a Man* if you watch it thoughtfully. One of the things you realize is that it's not just professional comedians and "funny people" who struggle with the Joker Mask. Ray's film crew was constantly cracking jokes too. The boxing champ Vinny Pazienza was riding Ray with physical threats masquerading as jokes. The friend who helped him with his wardrobe makeover lobbed an arsenal worth of jokes at the women who judged Ray harshly for his (lack of) masculinity. In each case, the humor and sarcasm employed were obviously, if also unconsciously, designed to deflect from feelings of awkwardness, embarrassment, anger, and sadness.

Even the most serious guys can use humor as a mask. A paper from Raymond Tucker and a team of psychologists at Oklahoma State University described how "self-defeating humor," another term for self-deprecating humor, can be a sign of depression:

> Humor becomes a way of building barriers between us and the world around us. At first, it feels like protection, but over time, it becomes isolation and we end up living on an emotional island.

Robin Williams and Ray Harrington are part of a special group—comedians—who are most experienced with this kind of thing. Two days after Williams's suicide in 2014, the health writer Alexandra Sifferlin published an article in *Time* magazine called "The Psychology of the Sad Clown," in which she examined the question of the link between depression and humor.[4] She cited the world of Gordon Claridge, an Oxford University experimental psychologist, who ran a study on more than 500 comedians to determine what made them tick. His conclusions were striking: **"The creative elements needed to produce humor are strikingly similar to those characterizing the cognitive style of people with psychosis—both schizophrenia and bipolar disorder." Comedians, Sifferlin suggested as she summarized Claridge's work, "may use their act as a form of self-medication."**

In the 1980s, a pair of psychotherapists, Seymour and Rhoda Fisher, dove even more deeply into the matter. They figured that, if comedians did have psychological issues, there had to be a root. It couldn't just be a random thing. So they did exhaustive psychological profiles of 40 of the leading comedians of the time. The result was a book—*Pretend the World Is Funny and Forever*—that reveals the total and complete chaos that characterized the home lives of so many comedians. Indifferent parents, alcoholism, absent fathers, violence in the home—it was a swirl that demanded some kind of defense mechanism. "We would propose that a major motive of comedians in conjuring up funniness is to prove that they're not bad or repugnant," they wrote. "They are obsessed with defending their basic goodness."[5]

This research has led to some unexpected modern interventions. The Laugh Factory in Los Angeles is, inarguably, one of the world's most famous comedy clubs. It has played host to every big name in this business and has given many of the biggest their start. The owner, Jamie Masada, is like a comic kingmaker—some even call him the "comedy godfather." He is close personal friends with the likes of Dave Chappelle and regularly dispenses advice to both the titans of the industry and the folks just getting their start. But he was growing increasingly concerned about the mental state of many of these people he had put on stage. He counted Richard Pryor and John Belushi as friends, for instance, before they both gave themselves over to self-destruction. And he has seen too many comics come through his door carrying private demons the size of giants. After the deaths of Pryor and many of his friends, he decided to do something about it. "From Richard Jeni putting a gun in his mouth and blowing himself up [in 2007] to Greg Giraldo taking drugs and overdosing [in 2010], I just can't stand to watch all of my family, one by one [self-destruct]," he told the *Los Angeles Times*.[6]

So in the least likely place in the world—a comedy club—Masada inaugurated a four-night-a-week therapy program. The appointments were free, and two clinical psychologists were brought in to help. One of those psychologists noted that too many comedians she sees are using the laughter and approval from the crowd as a salve for some serious wounds. Masada is blunt and clear about it. He told *Slate* magazine, "Eighty percent of comedians come from a place of tragedy. They didn't get enough love. They have to overcome their problems by making people laugh."[7]

Masada's numbers may be more anecdotal than accurate, but you don't have to live in the world of professional comedy to see the basic truth of his statement. **It's not just that comedy can help people drown out their anxieties. It's also that comedy can be a tool to keep a certain distance from people.** Think about it: The class clown was the guy everyone wanted to be around, but he was also the one who seemed somewhat on his own. It was a strange paradox: People flocked to him to make them laugh, but no one was going to go to him when they were in a rough spot. He was the friend who could make you cry laughing, but you wouldn't call him if you actually needed a shoulder to cry on.

Thinking about this paradox and about Jamie Masada's therapy group reminded me of a man you've already met in this book: Tucker Max. Tucker got world famous for writing hilarious stories about his crazy, drunken sexual escapades. He sold millions of books, primarily to young men, but to legions of young women as well. Before I had Tucker on *The School of Greatness* podcast to talk about his publishing start-up, Book in a Box, and his dating book, *Mate*, I asked around to some mutual friends about what I should expect.

I'd heard that he was incredibly smart, that he could be tough and foul-mouthed and combative, but also that he was a hilarious storyteller—which made sense considering the books that made him famous. Person after person told me stories of being at dinners or events with Tucker and him telling stories that had the entire group rolling on the ground in hysterics. Sure he could be abrasive, but if you wound him up and let him go, at the very least, the interview would be a great time.

Our interviews were indeed a great time, but not for that reason. Tucker was serious, insightful, open, honest, and vulnerable. He delivered tons of value to my listeners and to me personally. It was a virtual 180-degree turn from the character I'd come to know in the pages of his bestselling books. He, of course, was hiding behind the Joker Mask too. All the crazy, funny stories about his debauchery and sexual escapades were a defense mechanism against a lot of pain and fear.

"Being close to people is hard for me. It's hard for a lot of dudes," Tucker told me. "It took me a long time to even admit that to myself."

I asked him how he made this turnaround, and he was his typical blunt, honest self in response: "I've been doing psychoanalysis for 3 years now, and what it really does is it just teaches you how to understand yourself, understand your emotions, understand where your thoughts are coming from, why you're having them, those sorts of things."

What Tucker was describing were all the feelings and the pain that the Joker Mask is designed to deflect and protect its wearer from. **"Being vulnerable is really scary," Tucker admitted. "That's why it takes real courage to admit your fears and to face them and to open up.**

That's really hard." How hard? Tucker is an incredibly strong-willed, strong-minded person, and it took him until his mid-thirties to finally muster the courage to rip off that Joker Mask and get to the core of all the unhappiness he was masking with funny stories about random hookups.

Tucker is incredibly gifted, and while he came from a family headed by selfish, divorced parents, he was fortunate enough not to grow up in the kind of poverty that affects the long-term economic prospects and mental health of so many underprivileged kids who deal with similar issues. In the wake of Robin Williams's death, a psychologist at the University of Illinois named Mikhail Lyubansky wrote a powerful essay called "Robin Williams and the Mask of Humor."[8] In it, one of the things that Lyubansky talked about was the time he spends each week working with incarcerated youth. He tries to teach them and get them to figure out that violence may not be the answer to their problems. And he does this by doing what many people do not do for these kids: He listens. He role-plays with them and tells stories, but it's his story of his work with these kids that is the most useful for our purposes:

> Over the years, I've met well over 100 kids. Some are so sad they are unable to utter more than a few words. Others are angry and resentful about being where they are, again. Another group tries to play it cool. Each type presents its own challenge, but there's another group that is harder to reach than any of the rest—the entertainers.

These are the kids who are the most eager to appear just fine. Life is all one big comedy to them, and they are the comedians. But there's a hidden life there too. He says:

These are the kids who have learned how to make others laugh. They've also learned that, in that comedic moment, they can temporarily forget about their incarcerated fathers, their abusive uncles, their substance-dependent mothers, and all the other troubles in their life. In that comedic moment, they hurt just a bit less. And so they grasp every opportunity to entertain and, in doing so, cover up the pain.

When he presses them and tells them flat out that they seem to be sad, they are quick to respond, "No, I ain't sad. It's all good. I'm good." Lyubansky is well trained enough to see the pain they're hiding, and his warning is for anyone who is a parent, guardian, teacher, or caretaker of these kids: **"The ones who are silly, that tell nonstop stories and jokes? They may be struggling more than most."**

To any guy, or maybe to anyone who has dated a guy, this isn't too hard to understand. I certainly do. I hide things. I keep things to myself. And when really pressed, maybe I'll use a joke to defuse the tension. There was a study done of how men and women react to movies, and the results were revealing. "Men experienced the same emotions as women when watching several films; however, they did not express those emotions the same way as the women in the study," wrote psychologists Ann Kring and Albert Gordon.[9] In other words, even something as neutral as movie watching reveals just how different men and women are when it comes to revealing emotions.

Those gender differences matter, even if we don't like to admit that they do. I know many women who could make a room burst out laughing, and I also know they are using those moments to conceal things. But for young boys, in particular, humor often carries a bit of acid with it. It's part of how young boys are socialized and grow up.

When I spoke to Niobe Way, who is a professor of applied psychology, the codirector of the Center for Research on Culture, Development, and Education at New York University, and the president of the Society for Research on Adolescence, she told me that the joking mask is the one she sees most often among boys. "Boys often tell me that their best friend is their best friend because he doesn't laugh when something painful happens. In fact, if you can't take a joke, that's a way of challenging your masculinity." This isn't just research or work for her either; it's personal. She has a son, and as she told me, her attention to the Joker Mask is acute in only the way a mother's could be:

> *Everything is a joke to him and his so-called friends. Like all boys, my son is incredibly sensitive, and in sports, boys say incredibly, unbelievably mean things to each other, and what he's learned how to do is just take it, because if he doesn't take it, he gets mocked even more. These are close friends, supposedly, and they're mocking you about the thing you're most insecure about. My son never cries, because even being raised by a mom like me, he's so wound up. He'll tell me about someone saying something that just cuts to the root of his massive insecurity about a physical attribute or something, and I'll point out how mean that was. He'll say, "Mom, he was just kidding." I'll reply, "Did you think it was funny?" I know he's saying that they're joking, but I also know there's no way he thinks it's funny, so what he's really saying is*

*that he can't think it's not funny because then
they won't be his friend.*

What Niobe Way is describing is, to most guys, something we like to call "busting balls." It's almost a competition to see who can say the meanest things to each other. We mean well. We aren't trying to hurt each other, but it's also undeniable that we are because what we are doing is reminding our friends that we know the thing that they are almost always most sensitive about.

I agree with her. **In my experience, the people who make fun of someone else are really deflecting their own insecurities onto that person.** *Hurt people hurt people.* I used to be made fun of a lot. I was the young guy on the sports team, which made me an easy bull's-eye for jokes, and I took that frustration out on being a better athlete so they couldn't make fun of me. But they still did. There were times I did the same thing to other kids. I was trying to push the attention away from myself and put it on someone else so I didn't have to experience that humiliation.

"The Joker Mask is so frustrating," Way admitted in our conversation, almost exasperated. "The level of abuse, my god." And the worst part is: We rarely talk about it. As she pointed out, we talk a lot about the Sexual Mask. We talk a lot about male aggression. We talk a lot about these things because papers are published on these matters and then those papers filter into the media, where they take on a life of their own. People lead campaigns on these issues, and talking heads love nothing more than to make big causes out of them.

But joking? Who doesn't like a good joke? Who is going to lead an anti-joking campaign? But what happens when jokes cut too deep and we don't say anything? When we say we're just "busting a guy's balls," do we know if we're causing him actual damage? When we are "just teasing," what if we're actually hurting them instead?

Sometimes joking isn't about making fun of someone, it's about making fun of a situation to disconnect ourselves from whatever uncomfortable emotion it creates in us. Guys in particular are great at this. An awkward moment will settle in . . . and someone will crack a great joke, just to ease the tension. There will be some great emotional moment, and instead of just honoring it and sitting with it, some guy will have to pretend to fart or call another guy a funny name. Eric Hyde, an online writer who runs a blog on psychology, articulates this well:

> *Humor always allowed me to engage in relationships without risk. Using humor, I was able to derail conversations before they ever got too deep, thus keeping people at arm's length; keeping them at a safe distance emotionally. Unfortunately, this behavior continued into my marriage (unwittingly) and became a barricade to intimacy.* One of the things I desire most in life—true communion with my wife—was being frustrated by my subconscious fear of vulnerability, displayed by way of humor.[10]

The Joker Mask becomes our way of avoiding whatever emotion it is that we're meant to feel in that moment.

What's the effect of all this? A culture of closed-off, unavailable men. A culture of men committing

suicide at astonishing rates compared to women. The United States has the highest male-to-female ratio in suicides of any Western society. It is estimated that for every one woman who takes her own life, six men commit suicide. Men are living lives disconnected and closed off from sources of meaning and self-worth—things like friends, family, community.

For boys, the culture of scathing jokes and emotional disconnection can spill over into conflict. Remember that we often don't wear just one mask, but multiple masks. When the Joker Mask isn't enough of a defense, the Aggressive Mask might take its place—he might try with sticks and stones what words couldn't manage. I'll tell you, most of the fights I've seen or heard about were provoked by a remark that pressed the wrong button, or they were incited by teasing that went too far. Someone finally had enough, and then *bam*.

Niobe Way, in her research, adds this striking fact: "Exactly at the age that we began to hear the language, the emotional language, disappear from boys' narratives—in that National Data, that's exactly the age that boys begin to have five times the rate of suicide as girls."[11] She's not saying, of course, that acting like a joker can lead to suicide, but she is suggesting that getting distant from your inner emotional life can be a truly toxic thing.

And that's what the Joker Mask is about at bottom: It's about building a little cocoon of comedy around yourself so that you can avoid whatever emotion it is you don't want to experience. In many cases, with young boys, humor is used to avoid seeming too feminine. As Niobe told me:

[Boys] really buy into a culture that doesn't value relationships, emotions, empathy, all these things that we've feminized. So boys begin to devalue their relational parts to themselves, their relational needs, their relational desires. And they enter into a culture of masculinity that makes these bizarre equations where male intimacy has to be about sexuality (because it can't be about friendship). They start saying things like, "I feel close to him, no homo. He's cool, no homo." They make these constant allusions because any sign of intimacy is going to be perceived as potentially gay. Their understanding is that if you're straight, you have no desire for male intimacy. We don't do that with women, we only do that with men.

Let me be clear on something. The world needs more humor, laughter, joy, and positive expression. There is so much pain, suffering, fighting, and miscommunication that cause these negative emotions, feelings, and insecurities. So more than ever, we need joy and wholesome humor. There's nothing wrong with making jokes, making light of something, being playful with people, as long as it's not intended to hurt someone. There's nothing wrong with trying to be happy all day long, as what we're all striving for is to live happy, fulfilled, meaningful lives.

But if you did a "self-audit" about your use of humor and sarcasm, what do you think it might reveal? Would it tell you that you're avoiding a conversation you need to have, or a tough emotional moment that you don't want to face? Would it tell you that you're deflecting or derailing? I can't know for sure, but I'd encourage you to see if there's something beneath the jokes. My guess, based on my own life, is that there is.

| WHAT CAN WE DO RIGHT NOW? |

Having a sense of humor is not a bad thing, but there's a time and place for everything. When you're using humor as an avoidance tool, it becomes detrimental. When you're using it to add fun and joy to a situation, it works. If you're one of the many men who struggle behind the Joker Mask, knowing when you're doing one or the other is difficult at first. However, if you are someone who is always joking, you can be virtually certain that you are one of those men who are always sad, always trying to avoid, and who use their sense of humor because they feel they have no sense of credibility. Nothing could be more detrimental to the achievement of extraordinary results that so often come with greater intimacy and authenticity.

What's Available When You Drop This Mask (Joker)

Remember Joker Man, you are a gift, and there's so much to celebrate about you. The people who care about you the most have been waiting to see what's behind your mask. It's time to reveal the real you. These are some of the things that can flood back into your life when you drop this mask.

Deeper relationships

Worthiness

Richer experiences with others

Acknowledgment of all your gifts

People taking you seriously

Healing

Connection

Feeling enough

MEN:

Give yourself permission to feel and connect, as not everything is a joke. There's a time to tell the truth, to be serious. Connect to the people who surround you, the environment, and the mood. Starting today, whenever you are in a social situation or in a serious conversation, stop yourself before you make that joke that's sitting on the tip of your tongue. Ask yourself: Is it appropriate to be laughing in this moment? What information—factual or emotional—is being presented to me by the person or people around me? What am I trying to avoid? Is it the truth? The past? Pain? Fear? If you're present and connected all the time, eventually you'll know. Be emotionally conscious in all moments.

WOMEN:

The next time he pulls on his Joker Mask, stop him. Have a heart-to-heart with the man in your life who does this and let him know how you feel when he turns everything into a joke. Don't get angry at him or make him feel wrong for his humor, otherwise you may push him away. Instead, let him know, in a loving way, how it affects his credibility, your desire for intimacy, or a future together. Share what you want from him in specific terms, because you may be the first person who gives him the language to describe the emotions and the pain that the Joker Mask has been separating him from all these years.

THE INVINCIBLE MASK

No man is invincible, and
therefore no man can fully
understand that which would
make him invincible.

—MIYAMOTO MUSASHI

ANY LIST OF the most badass humans on the planet would surely have to include Travis Pastrana. His feats are, at this point, almost too many to count. He has jumped out of airplanes without parachutes. He was the first person to ever do a double backflip on a motorcycle—and first to land one in competition. He has done ramp-to-ramp jumps in cars, over distances that make your eyes bug out of your head. Just go to YouTube and type in "Travis Pastrana." You won't believe what you'll see.

Like Evel Knievel, Travis has paid for it—in the currency of punishment to his body. As one article reported, "His laundry list includes dislocated spine, in his left knee he's torn his ACL, PCL, LCL, MCL, his bucket handle meniscus, he's broken his tibia and fibula, he's had surgery on his left wrist twice, left thumb once, two surgeries on his back, one on his right elbow, nine on his left knee, six on the right knee, one shoulder surgery which left him with the only piece of metal he has in his body."[1] And that's just the short list. He has put it all on the line so hard, so many times, in so many ways, that each fresh feat seems just to confirm to the world what we already know: He's crazy. To put this in perspective, there was a film made about him called *199 Lives*—because it seemed that he could only have done what he had done if he had been able to cheat death just that many times.

I had a chance to talk to Travis on my podcast, and for someone who seemed to treat death as an afterthought, he had actually thought quite a lot about it. In fact, it seems that from a very young age he's been aware of his own mortality. As he told me in our interview, "When you're 15, and not to say that you're going to take huge risks, but you're going to say, 'Okay. You know what? I might not make this, but if I do, it's worth it.'"

That attitude has created a bold and lucrative career—but it's also meant that he's never gone a single year without a significant injury. Travis also talked to me about friends who have died or friends who are living with life-altering injuries. As Travis put it about a friend who had been paralyzed, "When they lose what their whole life has been about, their whole passion . . . what do you do when all you did your entire life was ride your bikes and run and then you can't walk anymore?" It was a question that hung in the air during our conversation. **What happens to you when the feeling that nothing can go wrong goes away?**

Pastrana was candid that some of this feeling of invincibility was driven by his own competitiveness. "Because if you want to be the top at whatever you do, if you want to excel at whatever you do, you make mistakes. You're going to push yourself a little past," he said, echoing something I've felt myself. If you're a competitor, if you're an athlete, if you like to win, you're willing to accept some risk, even if it means an occasional trip to the emergency room. I know in my own life I've pushed myself way past acceptable limits. In football, especially, you put your health (specifically your head) on the line every time you step onto the field.

But guys don't quit. Guys don't give into fear. Guys push themselves a little past whatever is reasonable and safe. That's the lesson we're taught when we're young, not only from our parents but from watching famous people like Travis on TV. We want to be like those cool guys, so we try to do what they do—whether it's jumping off the roof into a pool, fooling around with drugs or guns, or getting into fights.

But at some point, you start to wake up to some of these feelings. You start to realize that, "Hey, I'm not as young as I used to be." Or, "Hey, my body isn't supposed to feel like a used punching bag all the time." Or, more seriously, "Hey, the things I'm doing to myself affect more than just me."

In recent years, even Pastrana has come to accept that his feeling of his own invincibility may not be entirely positive. Pastrana has a wife now and two kids—and his family has made him wake up to what he was doing to his body. "I'm alive, I've got two kids, family. I like my life. I'm pretty good," he confessed. But it wasn't just his family. It was also the recognition of his own mortality. He talked at length about a friend, Erik Roner, who was killed in a sky-diving accident:

> *We lost Erik Roner last year, which was really, really tough. You know, he's got two kids, he had slowed down so much, and he was just . . . he was our safety guy. He was a guy that came on that was like, "Okay, nope. This is too windy." And he would pull everyone back . . . And I have that guy, that mentality, someone that loved his family so much, that would have done anything. You know, he was working so many different things to stay in the industry, in the sport, and he dies on a skydive, not even a base jump, and that really took our whole community back to say, "Okay, you know, you warm up with a backflip in the morning, but you're still 40 feet off the ground with a 220-pound motorcycle over your head, you know, make sure you turn the gas on."* It's the stupid stuff, it's like it's every day to us, but nothing can be taken for granted. Even driving to work every morning. You never know.

It isn't popular to talk about these things, especially in the communities in which Travis does his work. I have a lot of respect for the fact that Travis is willing to talk about taking his hand off the throttle a little bit—that he's willing to admit where his line is—because it's probably better for his brand to talk about the latest trick he did or the biggest stunt he's pulled off. He'd seem cooler if he pretended he was utterly fearless. If the world thinks you're invincible, and they're willing to pay you for it, why not keep up the image, even if it feels more and more like fiction?

Talking about death? *That's for wusses and sissies.* Except Travis Pastrana is anything but. Ask any man, and they'd say Travis has punched his man card. He doesn't shy away from any challenge. And now, in conversations, he talks about his sense that life isn't endless and that some risks might not be worth taking. **What Travis has done is take off his Invincible Mask. He's come to terms with the fact that life gives you only so many chances, and that, yes, you should take them, but no, you shouldn't press your luck—especially when luck, not skill or experience, is what will most likely determine success or failure.** Which, in Travis's case, could often mean life or death.

This has made him not only a better man, I would argue, but it's made him a better athlete and businessman, too. Kevin Feige, the president of Marvel Studios (who knows a thing or two about superhero thinking), explains why: **"If you start thinking you're invincible, you start making bad decisions."**[2] **He means that in business, in sports, in life, if you think there will never be consequences for your decisions, that you can just take risk after risk after risk, eventually you will attempt something that jeopardizes everything you've built.** You'll be reckless and dumb. If you think no one can touch you, just wait—someone will and it will be very painful.

When we're young, we don't think about our own mortality, because we're foolish, and death seems like an impossibility. We think there's no cost to pushing ourselves in this way. Terrell Owens, one of the NFL's greatest wide receivers, said this: "People forget that I'm a human being, just because I play a sport that everybody loves. We're human. We're not invincible. We share the same feelings and emotions that people on the outside feel. I don't think people really understand that."[3]

The same is true for the people you see on the *Forbes* list of billionaires or the musicians you see on stage. Or, closer to home, just because your father or your grandfather seemed to be so unflappable and strong doesn't mean that they aren't human too. **Just because someone seems fearless and brave and untouchable doing what they do doesn't mean they are. But when we're aspiring, when we're at the bottom looking to make it to the top, sometimes we try to mimic how we perceive people at the top act. This is when we unconsciously put on the Invincible Mask.** We're pretending. And in the process, we are putting ourselves at grave risk.

Unlike any other mask men wear to hide their fear and vulnerability, the Invincible Mask is the only one that can truly embolden men to commit acts of reckless stupidity. These are acts that affect not just their own physical safety or their own mental, emotional, or financial well-being, but also affect the people around them and closest to them. In fact, this behavior can start very young. I've fallen victim to this myself. I know how hard it is to get the Invincible Mask off once you feel like you can get away with anything.

From age 9 to 13, I fell down a rabbit hole of dishonesty

that began, I believed, because I was such a slow learner and an even worse test taker. I would start my homework as early as possible when I got home from school, and I'd study countless hours to prepare for a test, yet it never made a difference. I would always fail. I started worrying that I might get held back, which is the ultimate humiliation. So I started cheating. It began with homework with friends. Then it turned into peeking over shoulders during quizzes, which turned into full-blown cheating on papers and those multiple choice Scantron tests.

I felt bad in the beginning, and I was petrified that I would get caught and the school would tell my parents, who would be totally devastated. The thought gave me a pit in my stomach. But I never got caught, and over time I realized I never would be. **I got so good at cheating that I didn't even bother pretending to put in all those hours of studying that used to lead to a dead end. I felt like I could get away with almost anything, and that led to something even worse—stealing.**

Now cheating was one thing. Yes, I was breaking school rules, cutting corners, and doing things that could get me suspended or expelled depending how far I took it, but I was only hurting myself; I wasn't hurting anyone else. Stealing involved more than breaking the school's rules; it involved breaking the law. It involved taking from someone, which could hurt their livelihood.

Like the cheating, the stealing started small. I would take packs of cigarettes because I wanted to show off to another boy who smoked that I could get him a pack. Once I realized I could get away with that, I started stealing candy bars and magazines. Then my feats got bigger and more advanced. I took clothes, CDs, even expensive jewelry—not "thousands of dollars" expensive, more like $100 jewelry. As a 10-year-old in 1993, to me the risk felt high enough that I might as well have been robbing diamonds from Tiffany's on Fifth Avenue. I didn't care. Nobody was going to catch me.

It got so bad that it became an addiction for me. Every time I went into any store, I had to steal something. Most of the time it was a pack of gum or a couple of candy bars or a pack of baseball cards, though on the rare occasion I'd take a hundred dollars' worth of stuff just to feel the bigger high. **For more than 2 years, whether it was a gas station, card shop, grocery store, candy store, convenience store, or shopping mall, if I went inside, I took something. And I never got caught.**

Then one summer day when I was 12 years old, my dad was taking a basketball teammate and me to an activity somewhere when he had to stop by a client's home on the way to finalize a new life insurance policy (my father was a life insurance agent for 32 years).

His client lived on a farm in the middle of nowhere. And seeing as it was hot and he needed at least 30 minutes to go over some paperwork, my dad brought my friend and me inside to meet the man and stay cool. While they talked a few things over, we thought it would be fun to walk around the house and check it out. Like any curious kids in a strange house, we eventually ended up going down into the basement. This wasn't the creepy type of basement though; it was the finished kind that looked like a home office space. There were some file cabinets and an old desk with drawers and a lamp on top of it. We turned the lamp on, and like a good thief, I started going through the drawers. You never know what kind of valuable stuff might be hiding in certain places. We didn't have to search long to hit the jackpot: Sitting right there in the top drawer was an unsealed white envelope with $25 inside.

It was a golden opportunity. If we didn't make any noise and snuck outside like we were just hanging out, no one would know it was us who took the money. My friend took the $20 bill, I grabbed the $5 bill, and we headed up the stairs. Even at the time, I remember feeling guilty and conflicted about what we were doing. On the one hand, I wanted my teammate's acceptance. On the other hand, I didn't want to do something to make my father look bad. **Unfortunately, neither of those feelings mattered, because the invincible thief voice in my head took over and reminded me that worrying was stupid because I was never going to get caught.**

I went to bed that night like it was any other night; I was just five dollars richer. Then, around 4:00 a.m. I felt a large presence sitting on my bed. It was my father. He woke me up and explained that the man I'd met earlier that day had just called to tell him he was missing $25. It was money he was planning to buy fertilizer with for part of his farm, but when he went downstairs to his office, he discovered that the money was gone. Now my father was very loving, but he was also a pretty imposing figure, so if he wanted to, he could intimidate the crap out of me.

"Did you and your friend take it?" my dad asked, staring right through my Invincible Mask and into my eyes as he loomed over me.

"No, I didn't take it. I have no idea what you're talking about," I replied, as any good thief would, covering his tracks and playing dumb.

"Don't lie to me, son." He could see right through the

mask, I realize now. "Did you take the money from my client?" Again, I said no—half out of tiredness, half out of fear. I honestly didn't know what would have happened if I said "yes" right then, and I was too scared to find out.

It didn't matter, because I was going to find out anyway. Later that morning, my father approached me with an incredibly angry look on his face: "You lied to me, Lewis! I talked to your friend's mother, and he admitted to her that you boys took the money."

I was devastated. All the guilt I had kept suppressed with this Invincible Mask came pouring out. My friend had unintentionally ripped this mask off my face by doing the right thing. I was overwhelmed by the shame I had brought on my father and my family—not just with this incident, but with all my other instances of cheating and theft. My dad worked his butt off for my mom and his four kids. He already had one son who had just gotten out of prison for selling drugs, and now his other son was making stupid mistakes that could land him in jail as well?

It was too much, and neither he nor my mom was going to let me off easy for it. They drove me back to the farm that same day. The car ride was the longest hour of my life. Silent the entire time, I could see the fumes raging from my father's ears. I begged them to not make me do it, but they knew that if I didn't own up to my theft directly and face the person I victimized, I would likely find a way to rationalize my behavior and slide back behind the mask that got me here. So I got out of the car, took the money, and walked what seemed like a mile over to my dad's client. In the movies this is the moment where the older, wiser man accepts the money from the apologetic, misguided young boy, pats him on the head to make him feel better, and everyone learns a lesson. But life is not a movie. This farmer had the most agitated look of disgust and anger on his face toward me. I handed him the money, said I was sorry for stealing, and walked back with my head down and my tail between my legs. He didn't want to hear a word I had to say. He was a man who grew things in the earth to feed his family, and I had literally threatened the growth of his family and his business.

I'm not sure what happened to my father's business relationship with the farmer, but it's very likely that my naive, immature sense of invincibility cost him a lot of money. I paid for it by working my butt off all summer: chore work around the house, helping neighbors, and cutting greens at the local golf course every morning at 5:00 a.m.

After that day, I never stole anything again. Something had switched on inside me: I saw that this wasn't the path I wanted to go down. The Stoic Mask I had been wearing since my brother went to jail was holding back a tidal wave of emotions I didn't understand and couldn't control, but this cheating and stealing was the first time I felt like I was actually in control of anything. **The more I did it without getting caught, the more in control of my life I felt until, inevitably, I started to feel invincible. It was an incredible high, just not a positive one. And I wanted to change directions now.**

So I turned all this energy toward sports instead of stealing. It was unquestionably a better direction, though the idea that a change of direction alone would solve the problems was a total illusion. I was still hiding behind my masks. If we're honest with ourselves, those of us who want to achieve tend to believe we can do anything when we recognize mistakes and change direction (in business, we call that a "pivot"). In a way, that belief drives us to take risks and do bold things—but I think it's worth pausing to appreciate how much damage it can do if you ignore the underlying problems. **You can't just ignore the things you're doing to yourself, to your loved ones, to your body, to your mind, to your reputation, and to your sanity . . . because they will catch up with you.**

I find that this is particularly true of my driven male friends. What guy wants to acknowledge weakness and fear? It seems to me this is the primary thread that runs through almost every mask in this book. If only men could just admit they're afraid or insecure or in pain or that they need help. Want to understand why athletes are afraid not to play while hurt or injured? Or why they think they can beat the concussion protocol and keep going? Or why guys think that they can drag race on city streets and not get hurt or arrested? Why they think they—alone among men—will not have anything go wrong? The answers become clear when you understand the power of the Invincible Mask.

In the book *Men in Therapy*, Richard Meth says, **"The aggressive pursuit of power may produce prestige, authority, and money, but men rarely are aware of or even consider the negative consequences. External power frequently leads to self-neglect."**[4] He couldn't have put it better, and when I first read that quote, the phrase "self-neglect" hit me right in the gut. In all my years of achieving and doing, of taking big risks, I was neglecting myself. I wasn't taking care of myself in a way that allowed me to be at my best. I was singularly focused on each new challenge or fresh opportunity, and it led me to some dark places with negative consequences for my emotional health and my personal relationships.

But what I've learned is that it isn't just physical invincibility or taking extreme risks that creates problems for men. I don't want to make it seem like this issue is isolated to people who do dangerous work. It isn't. It affects anyone who doesn't have a sense of their own frailty or mortality or even their basic health. **If you push yourself past what is reasonable often enough and long enough, well, you might as well be chasing down tigers and base jumping off skyscrapers. Because your overwork can lead you to run the same risks.**

I talked to Jonathan Fader, who is one of the world's great performance coaches and psychologists. He understands that deep burning need to achieve excellence and how it blocks men from any sort of vulnerability, period. We talked about how profound that struggle is, especially for young men in locker rooms around the country:

> *Maybe your heart tells you that you should really focus on your relationships, and your heart tells you that you should stand up for certain values you have. But then you're kinda fighting against the predominant norm in our society. In the same way that someone who is trying to eat right is fighting homeostasis, or fighting all the delicious food that's out there. It's the same thing. You're fighting this chocolate cake that's everywhere. It's on every table, with the words "man up" spelled out in delicious, tempting sugary icing.*

Dan Harris knows about this too. Dan is a face known to millions. In 2004, he "had a panic attack on a little show we do called *Good Morning America*." More than 5 million people watched Dan basically break down, live. I had the chance to talk to Dan about his life and about his book *10% Happier*. The book has been a smashing success, selling thousands of copies and changing people's lives. But it began because of the worst kind of professional failure—a public one. One seen by many, many people:

> I was actually doing the news updates. I'd done the job many times, so I didn't have any reason to foresee that I was going to freak out. A couple seconds into my schtick where I was just going to read six or seven stories off the teleprompter, I just lost my mind basically. My heart started racing, my palms were sweating, my mouth dried up, my lungs seized up—I couldn't talk. I was supposed to be saying things and I couldn't even squeak out any noise, so I basically ended it. I tossed it back to the main host of the show and . . . If you watch it—a lot of people have watched it on YouTube—I get one of two reactions: If you've ever had any taste of panic in your life, you know exactly what you're looking at and it's very painful. If you haven't, people say, "Eh, it wasn't that bad." It doesn't really matter because for me I know it was the worst moment of my entire life, no question about it.

Dan had fallen victim to years of overwork. As a young, ambitious reporter with a type A personality, Dan had spent a lot of time in war zones. "After 9/11," he told me, "I went to Iraq six times, Pakistan, Afghanistan, the West Bank, Gaza, Israel to cover the Second Intifada." He returned from those experiences with PTSD, but his ambition and ego—and his feeling of his own invincibility—kept him from seeking professional help. I understood that choice. As a football player, if you admit that you got your bell rung, you're not going back in the game. As a reporter, if you admit that you can't handle another explosion, you're not getting that next big assignment out in the field. So instead of seeking professional medical help, Dan began self-medicating with cocaine and ecstasy. And it wrecked his life.

By his own admission, these wounds were self-inflicted. He *chose* to take on assignment after assignment. He *chose* to become a workaholic. But it's the kind of thing that can creep up on any of us. **We think we can just keep burning the candle at both ends because, well, nothing can stop us. And then we wonder why our friends and family have forgotten who we are. We can choose not to sleep and take pills and push ourselves to the breaking point. And then we wonder why we have a short temper and are tired all the time.** We essentially turn ourselves into machines, going all the time without stopping, and then we wonder why even a short vacation is intolerable.

Dan turned to meditation to cure his issues, and his book is what grew out of that experience. He stopped believing he was invincible and started paying closer attention to the thoughts in his head—including stuff that wasn't exactly pretty:

It was terrible. I had a full frontal collision with the voice in my head. Basically what you see head-on is that you're an asshole. I am a complete asshole. All I'm thinking about is "When is lunch?" "Do I need a haircut?" "What's my relationship with my boss?" The whole trick is to notice that they're just thoughts and let them go. We spend so much time enchanted by these stories we're telling ourselves, but they're just stories.

They're just stories. That's so true. They're not going to kill us. We don't need the armor of things like the Invincible Mask to defend ourselves from them. **Paradoxically, in hiding behind this mask, in pushing through, hitting it hard every day, ignoring the pain, we are the ones who end up giving these stories the power we're afraid they already have.** And that can have huge negative consequences both personally and professionally, as Dan Harris can attest.

I'm not saying you should sit on a rock or move to an ashram and give up on your dreams. A big part of my previous book and podcast, *The School of Greatness*, is about achievement and the joys and thrills of it. I'm proud of my achievements, just as my guests are proud of theirs. But what I am saying—and what my guests have taught me—is that it's important to pay attention to the costs. **It's important to remember that you are mortal, and that you have needs like sleep, healthy food, family, friends, and community—and that they can be ignored for only so long before ignoring them bites you in the ass.**

Donald Schultz has traveled the world filming and photographing dangerous animals of all shapes and sizes. If there's anyone I can turn to about how not to get bitten by a poisonous creature, it's a guy who, well, has been. Donald takes risks—big risks. And he has had friends who have done the same and lost their lives in the process. When you listen to a guy like this talk, you start to see how his senses have improved with age, how he has developed an intuition about when to walk away:

> Intuition is a huge thing that people have turned their minds and their backs on. If I don't feel something, I'll just walk away. *There's no video that's worth my life. If I walk into a situation and things don't feel quite right, I'm like, "Okay, what is wrong? Is this me? Is it someone else? Is it the situation? Why am I not feeling this?" If I can't quantify it, I can just be like, "I'm not doing it." I always think of things, funnily enough, from the point of view of testifying in court. "Well, your honor, it seemed like a great idea at the time. We're on the exit point, it's windy, and it's about to start raining. But we've done a 2-hour hike so we were up here, so we might as well try and jump because otherwise we have to hike back down." In retrospect, it's not even an option. These perceived pressures are not real.*

That's one antidote to the Invincible Mask: simply stopping and assessing your situation. Don is a guy who takes photos of extreme sports and exotic animals—and even he criticizes what he calls "Kodak courage." As he put it, "I've had friends who die trying to get a shot. Trying to film someone, they are not looking where they're going and they fly into a wall. For a video, it's just not worth it." Avoid Kodak courage. **Ask yourself if you're doing something because you need to do it—or if you're doing it because you believe you're Superman, or that you can't get hurt, and the bragging rights are worth the risk.**

Remember that the story you tell yourself about how you can keep going, how you have more gas in the tank, is just that: a story. You need to keep it in check. One of the most interesting practices that Roman generals carried out was called the memento mori. A successful general was given the parade to end all parades when he returned home from victory. Think of the Macy's Thanksgiving Day Parade times 1,000, and then some. The general would ride through the packed streets in his chariot, and people would praise his name, applaud, and throw garlands at him. He was the ultimate hero. Homes and businesses would empty out into the streets just to catch a glimpse of the procession. It was, for a general, the greatest moment of his life—and "triumphs," as they were called, were the greatest thing you could achieve as a military man in ancient Rome.

And at that moment, on that chariot, at the most incredible point of that general's life, there was a slave standing behind him whispering, *"Hominem te memento"* (Remember, you are only a man). There was a purpose to this: A general praised and fawned over like that might forget he was only a human being. He might become so arrogant, so dismissive, and so full of himself that he would risk ruining himself. After all, a sword cuts through human flesh the same way whether it belongs to the most famous general or the least experienced fighter in the brigade.

We have to remember that life is short. We have to remember we are men, not gods. It's okay to admit weakness, to be scared, and to opt out of stuff you don't want to do. Above all, we have to be able to take care of ourselves, to recognize that we are not invincible.

Thankfully, age does this partially on our behalf. As Travis said, he's not 15 years old anymore; and with a family and a career, he has a lot more to lose. So he doesn't take the same risks. As we grow and mature, the same thing happens to a lot of guys. Their youthful recklessness fades. They don't drive as fast, they don't stay out as late, they don't get as drunk as they used to, and when someone insults them, they may be able to laugh it off instead of throwing down.

It's the other forms of invincibility that I worry about. The overworking, the invulnerability—the stuff that leads to the panic attacks that Dan had. When you feel like the weight of the world is on your shoulders, beware. That weight can be crushing. Carrying that weight leads to heart attacks, to suicide, and to breakdowns.

We are men. We are not machines. We have our limits—physically, mentally, and emotionally. Ignoring them comes at great peril. Don't risk it—don't ignore the warning signs that the dam may soon burst.

If we refuse to accept that we are human, inevitably we will lose what makes us human. The football coach Ray Rhodes has a famous quote:

> At one time, you think you're invincible. This just can't happen to you. But when it happens, the reality sets in that you either change or you die. You realize you've got only one life.

Only one life. You shouldn't have to break your back to realize that. It shouldn't take a breakdown on live television to get you to realize that the only life you have is this one and that it's fragile. Don't throw it away.

| WHAT CAN WE DO RIGHT NOW? |

A lot of people—men and women alike—do extreme things and take big risks to get attention and to feel relevant in a world where they feel powerless. Sometimes, like me when I was younger, they do illegal stuff just to feel like they have control over something when they get away with it. **These adrenaline junkies are always looking for the next thrill. The more they get away with it, the more often the risks pay off.** And the more often extreme behavior does not have extreme consequences, the deeper the Invincible Mask attaches to their face.

What's Available When You Drop This Mask (Invincible)

Remember Invincible Man, you are a gift, and there's so much to celebrate about you. The people who care about you the most have been waiting to see what's behind your mask. It's time to reveal the real you. These are some of the things that can flood back into your life when you drop this mask.

> A fulfilled and healthy life span
> Deeper relationships
> Self-esteem
> True courage

The permission to just be and not constantly do

A sense of belonging

MEN:

The world doesn't revolve around you. There are people who love and care about you for who you are. So ask yourself these questions and write down the answers in a place where you will see them every day:

▶ What is valuable about me?

▶ What do I value about my life?

▶ What risky activities do I regularly engage in?

▶ What am I looking for in these activities?

▶ Can I get those things elsewhere in my life?

If you are one of those guys who need extreme adrenaline to feel alive, you are missing out on the fact that you can create that energy in your life without risking your life. When you've answered all of the above questions, take an hour during the next Sunday you have free and go to your local cemetery. Find the grave of someone who would be your age today if they were still alive. Sit in front of that tombstone and think:

▶ What are all the things they've missed in the time they've been gone?

▶ What might their life be like if they were still here?

▶ What would be possible for that person if they were still alive?

▶ Now, what if you were that person in the ground?

What you do affects everyone. That may feel irrelevant to you now, but it's not. The people in the ground are valuable. They're irreplaceable. They're fragile, mortal, and human. Just like you.

WOMEN:

The next time you notice his Invincible Mask, let him know how important he is to you and your family and friends. Tell him that you don't want to be at his funeral—whether from working himself to death or by jumping off a building, with or without a parachute. He needs to hear from you that his life matters to you, and that he's important and is neither invincible nor replaceable. Most important, he needs to hear that if he continues to be reckless, he'll end up either alone or dead.

Set clear boundaries with him, letting him know you're here to love and support him, but not to enable his reckless stunts. Remind him you're there for him, but not to pick up the pieces when he breaks himself and everything you've tried to build together.

THE
KNOW-IT-ALL
MASK

It's what you learn after you
know it all that counts.

—JOHN WOODEN

MIKE ROWE is a modern Renaissance man. Most people
know him as the host of the show *Dirty Jobs*, in which he
takes on all kinds of disgusting and messy manual labor
jobs across America. Here's how the show opens: "My
name's Mike Rowe, and this is my job. I explore the country
looking for people who aren't afraid to get dirty—
hardworking men and women who earn an honest living
doing the kinds of jobs that make civilized life possible for
the rest of us. Now, get ready to get dirty." Mike doesn't
mess around: He has worked on farms, crawled in sewers,

and done everything that most of us would never want to do even once, let alone professionally.

Though most people know him for his willingness to get dirty, what they don't know is that Mike is among the most interesting and broad-minded people around. He's been an opera singer. He's been a pitchman. He is an Eagle Scout. He sang in saloons. He's worked on trade policy issues and testified before the United States Senate. This is a guy who is rich, not only in knowledge, but in wisdom.

So when I invited him to appear on my podcast, my leadoff question was the one I had been dying to ask him: What's the one skill every human being should focus on and have? His answer surprised me. I figured he might say something like "learn to work with your hands" or "figure out how to persist." Or maybe he would tell me his secret strategy for building a huge brand.

No, his answer was about humility: **"Two ears, one mouth."**

I looked at Mike a little confused.

"In proportion," he continued, "if everybody listened twice as much as they spoke, I just have to think it'd be a lot less noisy. And if you knew that you only got to say half of what you normally say, you'd probably be a bit more circumspect about what comes out of your head. That's just math, two ears, one mouth . . . When in doubt, shut up."

Dang. Here's a guy who acquires more life experience in 1 year than most of us do in 10, a guy whose speaking fee is north of six figures, and who hosted one of the most popular cable television shows around, and the skill he is most passionate about is . . . *listening*? When I thought about it, it made perfect sense. On my podcast, if I am talking while I'm interviewing accomplished figures in sports, media,

business, medicine, fitness, you name it, then I am, by definition, not learning anything because the person across
from me with all the knowledge *isn't* speaking. **When I
shut up and let my podcast guests do the talking, only
then are they able to share their wisdom and teach me
things I didn't know.**

Have you ever noticed how people tend to fill the dead
time in a conversation or a meeting by rambling on about
some random topic? Have you ever watched someone you
work with try to impress the people around them by going
on a long rant about something you can't even pronounce?
Have you ever seen someone in an important setting suck
the air out of the room by making it all about them? They
always have a response, they can't let anything go, and they
have to show you how smart they are.

It's obnoxious, isn't it? Worse, no honest guy can critique that tendency in other people without also having to
look in the mirror and admit how often they've been
guilty of it themselves. I cringe when I think of those
moments in my own life. I can barely stomach thinking of
the opportunities I've blown or the fool I might have
made of myself. I think: What if I had just stayed quiet?
What if I wasn't so insecure or didn't feel the need to
prove I had something to say? How different could things
have been?

**I call this tendency—the need to fill the void with
the sound of your own voice—the Know-It-All Mask.**

Look, I get it. It doesn't feel good to look stupid in front
of others. I know because I felt that way nearly my entire
life. It feels much better to have all the answers to all the
questions and to have a line for every moment and a joke for
every awkward situation. Here's what's going through the

heads, either consciously or unconsciously, of the men who live behind this mask: *If I say something—anything!—smart at this meeting, people will think I'm smart. If they think I'm smart, they'll like me. Then I'll feel like a real man.* So you go into the meeting, and instead of listening to people, you play your script over and over and over in your head. You get yourself psyched up, and then you start talking. Maybe you did well, maybe you didn't. But I can tell you what you didn't do: You didn't absorb one thing from what the other people said. Have you ever been in a meeting or a social situation with a group of strangers and 5 minutes after you leave, you can't remember anyone's name? That's because your script drowned out their information.

Worse, it's all about overcompensating. We think that if we talk, no one will suspect that we have no idea what we're doing. It's like the line in *Eleven Minutes* by Paulo Coelho: "That's what the world is like: People talk as if they know everything, but if you dare to ask a question, they don't know anything."

Here's the thing: If we're being honest with ourselves, then we'd admit that none of us know anything. I think Coelho would even agree that nobody really knows what the hell they are doing. We're all just making it up as we go along. And that's one of the scariest vulnerabilities of all for men. We're supposed to have all the answers and know what to do. Not knowing equals weakness, and weakness cannot be tolerated. Why do you think our dads always got lost on family road trips? Why do you think they had Mason jars full of nuts and bolts and screws in the garage left over from all the furniture they put together? Because directions were for pansies. As a man, you're just supposed to know that kind of stuff.

This know-it-all tendency doesn't just have profound implications on our personal relationships, it can also affect our professional lives. As I learned listening to the debut episode of the second season of NPR's incredible podcast *Invisibilia,* which is about, as they say in the introduction, "the invisible forces that control our behavior—ideas, beliefs, assumptions, *and emotions,*" the two are often intertwined. The episode is called "The New Norm," and it's about whether or not it's possible to change a long-held social norm. The hosts tell two stories. The one that really brought this idea home for me was about an oil rig named Ursa and how the company that built it, Shell Oil, hired someone to teach their workers how to be more vulnerable in order to operate the rig safely and most effectively.

What made Ursa so unique was that not only was it the biggest rig ever built at the time, but it was also going to be parked way out in the middle of the Gulf of Mexico in *4,000* feet of water. And all of this was happening at a time—the late 1990s—when oil companies were just starting to explore drilling for oil in deep water. Everyone involved was literally and figuratively in uncharted waters. This was especially true for the rig workers, most of whom were roughneck tough guys who'd only ever worked on dry land or on smaller rigs in shallower water. Now they were being asked to fly out onto rigs that were two football fields long and to use technology they'd either never seen before or that was so recently invented it hadn't been used yet. But that wasn't even the problem Shell was most worried about. These guys were totally up for it. **The problem was that none of them would admit they might not know what**

they were doing or that, actually, they might not be totally up for it. As the host, Hanna Rosin, put it in her introduction:

> *Rig culture back then? Not for sissies.* There were unwritten rules of macho everyone understood and enforced. Like, don't question authority ... If you made a mistake, hide it. If you don't know something, pretend that you do ... Never appear weak. *If, for some godfor-saken reason, you feel an emotion rising ... swallow hard.*[1]

As you might imagine, that mentality could cause massive, costly, fatal problems on a giant $1.5 billion oil rig filled with technology its workers had never seen and parts they'd never handled. Hence, Shell's desire to break down those long-standing masculine barriers and get their workers to be more open about needing help.

The main character in the story is a man named Rick Fox, who got his start in the oil fields as a 23-year-old roughneck but had risen through the ranks at Shell to find himself, in 1997, put in charge of planning the Ursa project. It was a massive undertaking—one that only added to the stress he already felt (but had trouble talking about) both at work and at home, with his son Roger about to leave for college.

For Rick, the effort by Shell to make it safe to be vulnerable didn't just make him a better oil worker and leader, it made him a better father. Prior to the training initiative profiled in the story, "even at home, Rick lived by 'rig rules': Don't ask questions, never look weak." Roger tells a story that perfectly encapsulates the damage this macho, Know-It-All Mask can do:

The first time I heard the words "Phillips head screwdriver," he [Rick] said, "Go get me a Phillips head out of the shop," and I didn't even think to say, "Hey Dad, you know I've never heard that before. I don't know what you're talking about." So I went to the shop to look for something I had no idea what it was and felt stuck because I didn't want to be vulnerable.[2]

This small moment, and others like it, created distance between Rick and Roger over many years. This distance bred resentment in Roger, and then eventually anger toward his dad. And but for the intervention of a Shell-financed leadership consultant named Claire Nuer—a French woman in her sixties—who actually reached out to Rick, it could have ruined their relationship forever. **Instead, they're closer than ever because both men have learned how to remove their masks and be vulnerable with each other.**

Other men on the rig experienced similar personal transformations as a result of this process of learning to be vulnerable. It undoubtedly saved some marriages, and it almost certainly saved some lives—very literally.

My experience with the Know-It-All Mask was nowhere near as dangerous or scary, but it was just as threatening professionally. When I set out to write my first book on greatness, I figured it would be easy. I had achieved a lot of my athletic goals, and I had transitioned into building what most would call a successful business that brought in millions of dollars. I had a huge platform and lots of people who followed my work. Clearly, I had a lot to say about the topic—and I thought I had a lot to teach as well.

Yet I struggled. The proposal ended up taking years. The writing did not come easily to me. I couldn't get the tone right. Then I realized what was blocking me: I was pretending to be way smarter than I was. I was being egotistical. Who was I to lecture anyone on greatness? That's when I made my pivot on the book. I decided the book should be about the *journey* to greatness. **Although I knew quite a bit, instead of focusing on what I did know, I would focus on what I still needed to learn. I would be a student. I would ask questions. I would be, as Mike said, two ears and one mouth.**

I knew there were people out there who knew a lot more about greatness than I did. And so I went out searching for them, asking questions along the way about how they got to where they are and what made them tick. The "school" of greatness had questions at its foundation—not answers. I was there *with* the listener, as a fellow traveler, learning just as much as they did in the process of putting this community together.

As a company like Shell Oil and men like Rick and Roger Fox can attest, there is nothing scarier than a man who can't admit that he doesn't know what he's doing. But neither is there anything impressive about a man who thinks he has all the answers. In fact, both men are dangerous because they have stopped learning. There's a line by a Stoic philosopher, Epictetus, that says, "You can't learn what you think you already know." My breakthrough as a writer and podcast host came when I got comfortable with admitting my ignorance and admitting (to myself, mostly) that I may not be the smartest guy in the room.

This isn't, by the way, some modern discovery. The

ancients knew it too. Their writings are where men like Paulo Coelho or Mike Rowe learned the lessons they've shared with us. It was the philosopher Zeno, for instance, who said, "The reason why we have two ears and only one mouth is so we might listen more and talk less." Socrates was widely acknowledged as the wisest man of his age. For the thousands of years since Socrates walked the earth, people have studied him, emulated him, and memorized his quotes and thoughts. The entire Socratic method—the basis for, among other things, all law school education—is based on his philosophy of asking question after question until the questioner arrives at the truth. And yet, what did the wisest man of his era say about his wisdom? "I know that I know nothing." That's it. An intelligent man whom we have revered for millennia based his whole model of thinking on the idea that he knows nothing.

There's another secret here too: Know-it-alls are almost always the people who fail to persuade, even though it appears that persuasion is all they seek. Cheryl Strayed is a writer and a wise, experienced soul who has a popular advice column called Dear Sugar. She's been through everything: addiction, heartbreak, crushing defeat, and then, perhaps a bit unexpectedly, success as a writer of books that I think every person on the planet should read. Here's how she summed up the problem with know-it-alls: "My concept of an advice giver had been a therapist or a know-it-all, and then I realized nobody listens to the know-it-alls. You turn to the people you know, the friend who has been in the thick of it or messed up."[3]

I know someone who has been in the thick of it, who has messed up a lot. His name is James Altucher. He is the kind of person who has earned the right to say he knows some things. Just consider his life: He's built companies worth millions of dollars, and then lost all the money. He's been recognized as one of the liveliest writers out there on self-improvement and self-development, and he's been through divorces, depressions, and personal issues big and small. He's written bestselling books that sell hundreds of thousands of copies. He has what seems like an idea a minute, blogs once per day, and has inspired millions of people to kick-start their lives.

And yet, his secret superpower would seem to be his willingness to admit he knows nothing. **It's his openness about the failures in his life that has drawn people to him—and these have been huge failures.** Here's James in his own words:

> *When I built my first company in the '90s, I did everything smart until I did everything stupid.*
>
> *We built websites for entertainment companies. Bad Boy Records, Miramax, Time Warner, HBO, Sony, Disney, Loud Records, Interscope, on and on. Oh, and Con Edison.*
>
> *Then I saw that kids in junior high school were learning HTML. So I sold the business. $15 million. About a year later, I hedged and cashed out. Sold all my shares. The $15 million was now cash.*
>
> *I bought an apartment for millions. I rebuilt it. Feng shui! I bought art. I played a lot of poker. I began investing in companies. A million here. A few hundred thousand there. One IPO I put*

> *$2 million in at $20 and watched it go to $0.*
> *They made wireless devices for deaf people.*
> *Huge market.*[4]

And then poof. Just like that, $15,000,000 in cash was gone. Losing money isn't the problem. It's what losing the money does to us that is. James contemplated committing suicide. He felt his life was over:

> *I felt like I was going to die. That zero equals*
> *death. I couldn't believe how stupid I had been.*
> *I had lost all my friends. Nobody returned*
> *calls. I would go to the ATM machine and feel*
> *my blood going through my whole body when I*
> *saw how much was left. I was going to zero, and*
> *nothing could stop it. There were no jobs, there*
> *was nothing.*[5]

He called his parents to borrow money. He had literally zero dollars in his bank account. They told him no. Paying for college was enough, they said.

There are, as I see it, two responses to this kind of life-destroying catastrophe: One is to sink into a pool of self-loathing and self-hatred. And for a while, that's what James did. He gambled. He drank. He flirted with suicide. He didn't exactly stop working; he tried other ventures, wrote some books, and yet he never had the success he felt he deserved. He felt like he'd been screwed over or that he was a loser. Nothing was working for him.

But then he came out the other side and started sharing about his pain. He started blogging about his weaknesses. He was shockingly honest. He started telling the world,

"Hey! I screwed up and managed to get out of a pit of despair. Here's what I learned."

He didn't puff up his chest and tell the world that everything was fine. He didn't pretend like the wounds hadn't cut bone deep. He didn't hide from the mistakes that were his and his alone. He didn't pretend like he knew everything. And you know what? That honesty earned him readers. His writing blew up because it enabled people to see themselves in his struggles. And now, hundreds of thousands of people hang on James's words.

He could have, if he had wanted, bragged and boasted about the millions he made—not the millions he lost. He could've been the kind of guy who walks around pretending like he knows everything. But he didn't. Instead, he blogs about things he doesn't know. He admits to being ignorant and foolish—and people *love* him for it. Just look at a sampling of his headlines: "50 Things I Pretend to Know Now That I Am Nearing 50"; "Step-by-Step Guide to Make $10 Million and Then Totally Blow It"; "How I Broke Through My Own Mediocrity"; "The Power of Broke"; "I Don't Know Anything"; "I Don't Know How to Be a Good Father."

What can we take away from his story? That there's virtue in the kind of authentic humility that James shows. Admitting you don't know things isn't weakness; it's strength. And it strengthens you because it opens you to information and experience that, when you combine them, become wisdom.

Consider that the next time you open your mouth. Consider it the next time you're in a meeting and you're tempted to "offer your two cents" even though, deep down, you'd actually pay a king's ransom to know what any of these people are actually talking about. Or better yet, consider how much you might learn if you just stopped and kept quiet. You don't have to pay anything; you just have to pay attention.

Successful people realize how little they know. Know-it-alls aren't just annoying because of the way they walk around making everyone else around them feel stupid. They're also fools. They're the kind of people who reject new learning for fear of seeming like they didn't know anything.

This hit me powerfully during one part of my conversation with Mike Rowe. He was telling me about an episode of *Dirty Jobs* where he found himself working alongside someone whose job is—brace yourself—castrating lambs. Yes, that's a job, and yes, someone's gotta do it. Now, for a while, Mike had been on the receiving end of a lot of criticism from various humane society–type groups for the other things that had appeared on his show. He'd go off and do an animal episode, and then boom, the letters and angry calls would pour in. So this time, he decided to head those people off at the pass. He asked the humane society what they think the right way is to castrate a sheep. They told him, "You take a rubber band and you put it around the testicles of the sheep." Over a couple days, their testicles will fall off.

When Mike got to the ranch and met the ranchers, Albert and Melody, he had a different experience. Here's what happened, in Mike's own words:

> *Albert reaches in his pocket and pulls out one of those rubber bands, you know, like the Humane Society told me, except it's not a rubber band, it's a switch blade. He pops it open and he leans down and he grabs the scrotum and he pulls the scrotum toward him, and he*

> *clips off the tip of the scrotum. And then he*
> *pushes the scrotum back, exposing both testi-*
> *cles, which look like thumbs on a little lamb.*
> *And then he bends down and he bites them off.*
> *And then he spits them in a bucket I'm holding.*

Yep, Mike watched a guy bite off a lamb's balls. He pushed back on Albert:

> *Albert tells me, "This is how we do it. This is*
> *how we've always done it." I'm like, "Okay,*
> *look. I don't know what kind of operation*
> *you're running here, but you're freaking me*
> *out. Can we just please do it the way the*
> *Humane Society does?" And he says, "Well, it's*
> *not very nice." Like, "Not very nice, you just bit*
> *the balls off a sheep, dude. Come on, man. Let's*
> *just do it right."*

So Albert, in deference to Mike, gets a rubber band and puts it around another lamb's testicles. The result? The lamb walks around, sits down, and trembles. It's clearly in pain. The rancher tells Mike that the lamb will be in that kind of pain for 2 days. Meanwhile, the other lamb, whose testicles Albert had bitten off, was walking around as if nothing had happened. For Mike, this was a big moment of insight: "It actually clicks in your head. And the lesson on that day was beware of experts, you know. Just beware of the idea that one size fits all."

Beware of experts. Beware of people who think they know about something but actually have very little experience.

There's a line from monk and teacher Shunryu Suzuki that expresses this insight succinctly: "In the beginner's mind there are many possibilities, but in the expert's, there are few." For Mike, the lamb testicle lesson was a powerful spur. It made him realize that, on his show, he didn't want to be a traditional host. He didn't want to pretend to have all the answers. Here's our exchange on how he changed:

Mike: I had become very facile over the years in creating the illusion of competence, but that's all it was. I used to call it the "plaque approach," like a plaque on a statue. So I used to host all kinds of shows, where, you know, we were pulling stuff out of our butt constantly. And I'd walked up to the statue of Francis Scott Key and I would read the plaque . . . get it in my short-term memory and then I turn around to the camera and I'd say, "Francis Scott Key, born in . . ." Right? And so, people will be, "Well, that Mike Rowe . . ."

Me: He knows everything.

Mike: Mike doesn't know shit. He knows how to read a plaque. And so, all of the ritualistic stuff from the hair, right, from hair and makeup, craft services, wardrobe, every single thing went out the window . . . **And what I was left with was the realization that I'm not a host or an expert.** *I'm a guest.* I'm an avatar for the viewer. And it's funny when you set the table

```
just  a  little  differently,  how  all
your  subsequent  decisions  will  become
informed  by  that.
```

Be a guest at your own show, Mike seemed to be telling me. And I've taken that advice to heart. I am probably more apt to listen now than I was before. It's also a lesson I've tried to apply in my life. I think it's something that everyone needs to do—but it's particularly important for men. **So many guys have inherited this notion that men are naturally superior, that we're kings of the world. It's crap, and it makes us act like jerks.**

Just look at the idea of "mansplaining": when a man—often less qualified than the woman he's talking to—explains something to a woman in a condescending way. That term absolutely nails something women have been putting up with for centuries, as Laura Bates from the *Guardian* explains:

> *Being corrected by less qualified men is a phenomenon reported by many women, particularly those with expertise in a male-dominated area. At the Everyday Sexism Project, we've heard from an IT worker whose less experienced male colleagues outline basic computer functions to her in meetings, an engineer who had a man try to explain solar panels to her, and a woman who dealt with a customer slowly spelling out her own company policies to her while calling her "honey."[6]*

There are whole Tumblr blogs dedicated to examples of mansplaining. Wise people have written long essays complaining about the practice. And while I don't want to throw myself into the middle of the gender wars, what I do know is that mansplaining is a branch on the same tree as know-it-all-ism. They are words almost exclusively spoken from behind the Know-It-All Mask. **As I hope this book has demonstrated so far, men can have deep wells of insecurity. And one of the ways we fill up that well is by showing off how much we know. We're especially prone to doing this—wait for it—in front of women.** But gender aside, it has the same basic flaw at its core: A human being who thinks he knows something going on at length to someone who might know something more than he does.

There's an old line by Ralph Waldo Emerson that I really like. He put it like this: "Every man I meet is in some way my superior; and in that I can learn of him." Galileo said something similar: "I have never met a man so ignorant that I couldn't learn something from him."

Everyone has something to teach you—if you're willing to learn it. If you're willing to close your one mouth and open your two ears.

But let's make sure we update those quotes for the 21st century: *Every person you meet is better than you at something, and you should make sure you learn from them.* Don't go around lecturing and talking down to people. Don't make assumptions. Don't fall prey to your own notions of expertise, or worse, your fears of appearing stupid and weak.

Instead, be humble. Humility is the virtue that allows you to become wise. When I think back, this is a trait at the core of the smartest people I know: They ask questions constantly, relentlessly. They believe that every single person has something to teach them. And they learn from everyone—from the guy who fixes their car to the CEO of a company.

The Know-It-All Mask is a particularly tough one to beat. Listening isn't a skill we're graded on. There aren't any national competitions for the best "listeners" (contrast that with the number of national speaking competitions). Superficially, illusions of knowledge can work well. There's that expression—"fake it 'til you make it." People trapped behind the Know-It-All Mask think that's what they're doing. They just don't realize how it's holding them back. It's impossible to know how much new music you're missing when you continue to sing the same old tune. If only there was a way to take inventory of how much know-it-alls are not learning when they've finished one of their typical conversations. If only they could see the impact they have on other people. Talking to a know-it-all—or rather, being *talked at* by one—is like going through the verbal equivalent of a meat grinder. It's exhausting.

It's time to have humility, a hunger to learn, and an openness to others. These are not easy qualities to cultivate. It's much, much easier and feels much, much better to walk around in the world wearing your knowledge on your sleeve. It's much more comfortable to go around saying "Here's the answer" instead of saying "I don't know" even if, like with old-school roughneck rig workers, it could get you killed. **And that's why the Know-It-All Mask is a mask: It covers up our ignorance and insecurity. It lets us walk around with a little bit of emotional armor in place, based on the little bit of knowledge we have acquired in our life.**

Want to be listened to? Want to have people hang on your every word? Hang on their words first. Listen to them—deeply. Pay attention to them—closely. **You'll find yourself** dropping your mask, being wiser for it, and, over time, being the guy whom people turn to when they need genuine advice. Because really, what people want most from their relationships with men—whether romantic or platonic—isn't a repository of solutions to all their problems; it's someone who will listen to them.

| WHAT CAN WE DO RIGHT NOW? |

Someone whose self-worth comes from his intellectual expertise, who cannot admit when he's wrong or when he doesn't know something, ultimately pays a heavy price in his relationships. True learning and connection become increasingly difficult as the Know-It-All Mask sinks deeper into their skin because all it does is create separation.

What's Available When You Drop This Mask (Know-It-All)

Remember Know-It-All Man, you are a gift, and there's so much to celebrate about you. The people who care about you the most have been waiting to see what's behind your mask. It's time to reveal the real you. These are some of the things that can flood back into your life when you drop this mask.

People want to be around you

Freedom to not know

Ability to learn and grow

Wisdom from others

Deeper intimacy

Support from others

MEN:

Practice listening. Be flexible in your point of view. Be open to new thoughts, ideas, and strategies. Try to absorb and understand new ideas even if you don't agree with them. **The one constant in the world is change. If you stay stuck in your point of view, you will limit yourself and your growth.** Empty your cup, as the Buddhists would say. Have a beginner's mind. It will help you relate to people and connect to them as a result. Doing this will bring more joy into your life than any amount of knowledge. And as Einstein famously said, "Imagination is more important than knowledge." People who hide behind the Know-It-All Mask often seem to be hiding from the idea that they might have a limited imagination.

WOMEN:

The next time he shows his Know-It-All Mask, be patient. When a man you care about mansplains to you, listen to him all the way through. Then, instead of responding to his arguments on their merits, share how it feels to be around someone who acts like an omniscient god, who must always be right. Make him understand what you are hearing with your two ears while he is busy running off with his one mouth.

Remind him what is important to your relationship and that it's better to be kind than to be right all the time. Let him know that you won't love or care about him less if he doesn't know something. Also, take time to explain your point of view; he might not have considered things from your perspective.

THE ALPHA MASK

> With the primal urge to be alpha comes extreme heartbreak. The harder we fight, the harder we fall.

—JOHN KRASINSKI

YOU'RE IN A BAR and some guy gets rude. You're in a meeting and someone other than you is getting all the attention. You're trying to talk your phone bill down, but the guy on the other end of the line is a jerk about it.

How does this make you feel? How do you respond? For a lot of men, the answer is simple: It challenges their very identity as a man. It makes them feel *less than*. Since they see themselves as alpha males—the top dogs—they simply cannot handle the downgrade in status.

But here's the danger—in some of the situations, the degree to which you are assertive and display your full alpha colors could meaningfully change what happens, for better or worse. It might affect whether you are able to walk away in one piece.

Chris Voss faced this kind of situation in the most high-pressure, high-stress environments possible. Chris was an FBI agent for 24 years and was the former lead international hostage negotiator for the FBI. He was the case agent on the Blind Sheikh case and the TWA Flight 800 catastrophe, and he was responsible for the surrender of the first hostage taker in the Chase Manhattan bank robbery. So when you look at the guys in this world who have had to figure out how to defuse alphas and deal with their tendencies, Voss may be one of the world's leading experts— and one of the only folks I know who has taken this specialized skill set and tried to talk to everyone about it.

Voss was a guest on my podcast, and he was by far one of the most interesting men I've ever had the chance to interview. I found him so interesting in large part because he forced me to rethink everything I thought about what it means to be an alpha. When I asked him about how you negotiate with the kind of person who has to win, who has to get everything he wants, who is very controlling, for whom it's his way or no way, Chris's answer was totally counterintuitive:

> *Well, getting everything they want is actually third on their list. First of all, being in control is number one on their list, and that's emotionally satisfying.* The second thing is the alpha

type—which we refer to as "the assertive"—
the one thing that's more important to them
than actually getting what they want is being
respected and making sure that you know
everything about what they're coming from.

So a hostage taker takes a hostage, makes a demand, but getting whatever they asked for is low on their list of things they want? According to one of the world's experts on the subject, what matters more is being in control and being the alpha. It's an interesting bit of insider information—I'm always intrigued to learn stuff like this—but that's not why it struck me so much. What struck me is what people like Chris Voss *do* with this insight.

Knowing that hostage takers or kidnappers crave respect and control is what gives hostage negotiators their edge. It's not about getting them $20 million in nonsequential unmarked bills or helping them get out safely on a fully fueled jumbo jet. That stuff is for the movies. And besides, the hostage takers are way too irrational to prioritize any of that. Chris successfully massages their egos and exploits as a weakness their desire to be seen as the alpha. While the hostage takers think they are in control and showing everyone how tough they are—that's precisely when Chris and his team are outmaneuvering them (sometimes fatally so).

In his bestselling book, *Never Split the Difference*, Chris talks a lot about how to negotiate—whether the issue is your cable bill or a raise from your boss. At the root of many of his strategies is that same idea: Let the other person think they're in control. Don't let your ego get in the way of doing what needs to be done. *Looking* like you're on top is not the same as getting what you want. Acting like the alpha is a waste of time.

That's the lesson for me. You might think you're the big tough alpha male, but you're actually pro-foundly weak. It occurs to me that establishing "alpha-ness" is what drives a lot of outrageous behavior and needless mistakes. When I think about things like gang violence or terrorism or bar fights or abuse, all of them seem to trace back to this need to establish one's presence or dominance or strength. All of these acts seem to be about men wanting to show off how alpha they are.

At the end of my first book, I tell the story of a huge fight I got into on the basketball courts near my apartment in West Hollywood. This incident propelled me to work with the leadership and emotional intelligence coach Chris Lee (whom I also worked with to start the *School of Greatness* podcast). I was nearly 30 years old when the fight happened, and I remember running back to my place after pummeling this guy's face bloody, flopping onto my bed, and nearly hyperventilating as memories of an equally bloody fight from my childhood flooded my memory banks. At the time, the two fights felt related. It was as if they tapped into a deep pain and anger that I'd never processed. You could say I'd stuffed these unprocessed emotions down and hidden them behind my Stoic Mask and my Athlete Mask. Upon reflection, I think all of that is still true.

But while I was writing this Alpha Mask chapter, that fight kept popping back into my memory. Something about how the fight went down kept bothering me. It wasn't the unmanaged emotional pain that had my attention; it was something else that I couldn't pinpoint. Talking to Chris Voss clicked it into place. What really tripped my trigger and had me seeing red on the court was that this guy was trying to dominate me. He was bullying me, trying to assert himself over me. His Alpha Mask was tied on real tight, and he was going to show me who was the big man on the court.

I'm sure the guy I fought is a decent man in his normal, day-to-day life. I bet he has friends and a mom who loves him. But I bet he also has a ton of emotional pain that he tries to cover up with his Alpha Mask. All his insecurities and fears probably melt away when he steps on the court with that mask on.

In the immediate aftermath of our fight, I did not feel great. I probably felt a bit of a rush. Maybe I felt powerful and strong and respected for a while. But now, several years after the fact, I realize how little I gained from that encounter and how much I risked.

Here's the truth: We misunderstand the whole alpha/beta definition. We tend to think of it as strong versus weak, active versus passive, hard versus soft, effective versus ineffective. All of that is nonsense. In most situations, we confuse strength with brutishness. We confuse being active with being directionless. And we confuse being hard with being insecure. A lot of what we think of as "alpha" behavior is simply a cover for hollowness. One of my podcast guests, former Navy SEAL and now governor of Missouri Eric Greitens, put it like this: "Arrogance is the armor worn by hollow men. Their bragging and puffery is usually just a display meant to mask their weakness."

The great executive coach Glenn Harris wrote a long essay about being a recovering alpha on *Your Tango* that spoke to the heart of this issue. **"Most Alpha men share the same deep insecurities. Their behavior, while posturing on the outside, is often focused on covering up their insecurities on the inside,"** he wrote.[1] In his personal experience as an alpha, and, he argues, that of thousands of others, alphas struggle a lot with their body image. "Alpha males often depend on their physical ability to dominate and compete aggressively against other male opponents. Alphas learn what it takes to physically rise above their competition. While alpha males probably won't verbalize this insecurity directly, male dissatisfaction with body image is approaching that of women's dissatisfaction."

For him, aging meant having to lose the parts of his body that gave him his self-worth. Losing his hair, his strength, and his waistline caused more than the usual amount of grief. And the ways that he, and alphas generally, compensate aren't so pretty:

> *Pressure mounts, as men age, to maintain our physical appearance and retain our competitive edge. Alphas often go to extreme measures (i.e., steroids, testosterone replacement, protein supplements, extreme sports, and excessive workouts), attempting to retain their place at the head of the pack* ... Alpha men often try to compensate for feelings of insecurity and loss through unhealthy extreme behaviors.[2]

He also argues that alphas have trouble with being vulnerable. "Most Alphas are insecure, self-centered, outcome-driven individuals who have little time for people and feelings," he wrote. **"However, vulnerability is a characteristic associated with authentic pride (considering yourself a person of value, not superior to others). Becoming appropriately vulnerable increases genuine humility and acceptance of oneself *and* with others, allowing them to see you as relatable and human."**[3]

This is not such a revolutionary concept, even though it is hard for so many men to grasp. Experts across various fields of study have arrived at similar conclusions. Jonathan Fader, a sports psychologist, talks about the effect of environment on people's behaviors in love and life. And one of the things he notes is how hard it is, in male environments, for someone to step away from the stereotypes:

> So in a locker room for a guy to step out and say, "Hey, listen, that's not right," or "Hey, I love you, man," or whatever it is that steps away from the masculine ideal, he's going against that strong negativity bias which just says, "I'm in danger if I step out of that norm." And that's a really powerful thing. And it takes an environment that's really supportive to that person to be able to do that.

Any guy reading this book has felt that pressure. Someone makes an off-color joke, and you stay quiet. You see someone getting picked on, and you look the other way. Someone is going through a tough time, and rather than offering him words of comfort, you change the subject or tell him to "be a man." There is that toxic phrase again. In other words, you act like an alpha because, well, that's what you're "supposed" to do with guys, right?

But imagine a universe in which boys didn't have to do that to each other. I don't mean in an abstract sense; I mean really think about a world in which boys didn't have to play a high-stakes game of alpha conquest to be able to spend time with each other. Imagine what that world might look like. Now think about how that would affect your own life. **How many behaviors have you internalized that were just alpha behaviors from when you were a kid, graduated to an adult level? If you're anything like me, I bet it's more than you're willing to admit. And that's what needs to change.**

It's not enough to say these things; you've got to live them. In my own life, I've stood on the medal stand and been named one of the best athletes in the country. I've set records. I've been in the gym and had guys watch out of the corner of their eyes as I ratchet up the intensity. I've been out with a girl and been recognized by fans. It's an incredible feeling. But it can't be what gives you purpose in life. This is not the jungle. We're not fighting to the death for status and respect here. It's mostly just ego.

I'm still an alpha in many ways—I hope in the good ways that are more about leadership and accomplishment than ego and putting others down. I still have goals I want to achieve. I go after them with energy and intensity. I still push myself, and I'm still looking for ways to be bigger and better than I have been in the past. But I think I've managed to round myself out in ways that help me in life, business, love, and friendships.

I'm also not saying dropping this mask is easy. **The fact**

is, guys don't sit around wanting to be alphas from when they're young. It's something that creeps in, and it often comes from the environment, as Jonathan Fader would tell you. Friends, popular culture, and all the other things that shape our identities are a potent cocktail that makes putting on the Alpha Mask feel intoxicating.

In doing my research on this subject, I stumbled across the dissertation of a PhD candidate named Christopher Taylor in the Department of Educational Leadership at Miami University. The title of the dissertation is "Bros Like Me,"[4] and it explores fraternity culture and what norms prevail in it. I found Taylor's paper to be incredibly useful, because if you think of frat culture, you're getting what is the equivalent of an espresso shot of alpha behavior. I'm not saying that's a good thing, but understanding something under a microscope can help you discover broader facts about the culture. So when Christopher Taylor examined frat guys, he found out some things that apply to males in society more generally. Here's one of his most interesting observations about what he calls "the guy code":

> The "guy code" is as follows: You must show a face that indicates everything will be fine, that everything is under control. *Winning is crucial when the victory is over other men who have less amazing or smaller toys. Kindness is not an option, nor is compassion. These sentiments are taboo, but are part of the rules that govern men's behavior in Guyland, the criteria that will be used to evaluate whether any particular guy measures up.*[5]

What's worse is that these criteria become social norms that lead to exactly the kind of behavior you'd expect—because like in all things, expectations lead to outcomes. What does this mean, and why should it matter to you? **Simple: If you wear the Alpha Mask too often and for too long, your behavior will start to change, and for the worse. What we normalize, we become. If you try to be an alpha for too long, you'll take on those characteristics.**

When I think back to my own alpha moments, fear is at their root. It's anxiety about my own situation, my own status—and usually it's based on the opinions of people who really don't matter to me in the end. **That's one of the peculiar things about the Alpha Mask. It's almost entirely something we wear because of the judgments of people who, in the end, don't really matter. Our family will rarely care how "alpha" we are; our true friends don't give a damn.**

But sometimes, society does. That's the tough part about this mask: It has certain rewards. Like a lot of masks, the alpha mask is rooted in insecurity and fear. But it can, unlike other masks, pay some dividends. Matthew Hussey, the dating coach I introduced you to in the Sexual Mask chapter, has helped literally thousands of people discover their partners, fall in love, and find lasting happiness. What's unique about Matthew is that while he started his career as a dating coach for men, he now works exclusively with women. He talked to me about how many men wear the Alpha Mask as a cover-up for their weaknesses with women:

> *It's a power play with women: I'm going to make*
> *sure you can never be as important as my*

purpose and my mission and my business. It becomes a way to always keep someone as a second-class citizen in your life. But it's not just status or someone who has achieved a high position and is getting off on that Alpha male tendency of "I'm-Always-Hustling, that's what I do: I go out there and I succeed no matter what." It becomes their sole source of validation. If you took that away from them, they'd suddenly feel worthless, like their life didn't matter.

Matthew continues, though, and is honest about why so many men behave this way:

Let's also not forget that, although men can be stupid, they are also not irrational most of the time. They have learned to rely on these things because they work. *Men get validated for being the tough guy. Men get validated for being bold and taking what they want. Men get validated for flaunting their money. People do these things not because they're stupid, but because on some level they work.*

But Matt is also honest about the mask's limitations. He compares it to building up only your biceps while letting the rest of your body become feeble and weak. If all you did was work on your biceps, he says, then you'd have chicken legs. And if all your validation was built up into the size of your biceps, then the minute you couldn't show those off, your confidence would fall like a stone.

In the same way, it's important to build up all parts of yourself. This is not something that is particularly

easy for men clinging to the Alpha Mask. After all, they put it on precisely because they are insecure about all those other parts. As Matt puts it, some guys' biggest fear is:

> *That ditching their old mask won't work. They want to stick with what they know. It's fear that the other muscles they are going to start building aren't going to pay off and the muscle they've already built is going to weaken. But the reality is that the more well-rounded you are, the more attractive you'll be.* Women are attracted to the guy who will be gentle with her and look after her and make her feel safe, open up to her emotionally and talk to her, while at the same time being a fighter when he needs to be. That's the guy who she thinks is a god. *What makes you a unicorn is not doing one thing really well, it's the combination of things that are all found in you that nobody else has.*

No one likes a one-trick pony. No one—women especially—likes someone who is basically just a big meathead all the time. No one is attracted to someone who is constantly stroking their own ego or endlessly comparing themselves to other people. Or, as Matt put it, "if you can only be masculine and win validation in one way and you're addicted to that way, then it limits you."

What does an evolved alpha look like? Well, my friend Brett McKay, who runs the site and podcast *Art of Manliness,* has spent a long time thinking about what an evolved man looks like. And when I asked him about it, he offered up a description based on the evolution he's had to make in his life, as related to becoming an alpha dad:

> *Having a family is a great opportunity for men to take the lead. And not just with your wife but with your kids as well. One thing I'm trying to do as a new dad is developing a mission for our family. It's been amazing. You have this chance to pass on values to your kids that are important to you. They're gonna be there after you're dead. It's very scary and humbling but also really exciting at the same time. That you can have that sort of influence on a person.* It's important to find ways to tap into sort of ancient man stuff that lies dormant in us in any way you can.

Brett's still being a leader. He's still taking charge. He's still making sure that his tribe is protected. No one would read that paragraph and think, "What a wuss. That dude's a beta." And that's the truth: We are not talking about overnight changes, or going from being all-alpha all the time to suddenly hanging it all up. What does have to change is your perspective on what it means to be an alpha and the ways you get those instinctive behaviors out.

To me, that's what the whole School of Greatness experience has been about. It's what *this* book is about. It's about evolution. It's about becoming more than you were yesterday. It's about setting goals and achieving them. But it's also about dropping a lot of the baggage that gets in the way. **If you're honest with yourself—and believe me, I've had** to do this—then you know that walking around puffing up your chest and acting dominant is . . . exhausting. After a while, even if it helps you in certain aspects of your life, it holds you back in others. If you put up that alpha façade, it keeps you from connecting with certain people. Real alphas don't need to do that.

Of all the people I interviewed on the podcast for this book, the one who understood this idea the clearest was Alanis Morissette. She's a really careful student of human beings and relationships. And she used a phrase during our conversation that's stuck with me since: the "empowered alpha." The idea is that being an alpha is as much about the effect you have on others as it is about who you are or what you achieve. As she put it:

> *When there's a negative connotation to alpha or beta, it's because there's a disempowered version of them acting out. So a disempowered alpha would be a misogynist, very dictatorial, not win-win . . . And an empowered alpha also turns to an empowered beta and says, "Here's what I'd want. Here's what I'd like to do. Here's the mission. How do you feel about that?" And the beta will go, "Genius," or "Let's tweak it a little bit," or, "Not feeling so good about that."*

Think of the best leaders you know, the ones whom you would characterize as alphas. I bet "alpha" isn't the first thing you think of when you think about them. I bet that you think about them as effective, kind, thoughtful, listeners—and yet, if pressed, you'd still call them alphas. **That's** the kind of evolution we're after—a place where people acknowledge, almost as an afterthought, that you're a strong, supportive, capable man. They don't have to see you chasing skirts or shotgunning beers to know that you are tough and manly and masculine.

So ease up on the Alpha Mask. Embrace a fuller view of what masculinity means. You'll find yourself more open to things and experiences and people; you'll probably have more adventures and connect with more women (and men). When he was asked about his greatest negotiating achievement, in a life filled with rescuing hostages and negotiating with terrorists, Chris Voss's answer was a testimony to what can happen when you remove the Alpha Mask:

> *Coming to a place where my son and I are working together better all the time. He works for me full-time, and that can be both wonderful and horrifying for both of us. I'm working really hard to respect him, to listen to him, and to value him. And he's working harder to not feel like I'm always trying to be the alpha male.*

| WHAT CAN WE DO RIGHT NOW? |

Nobody can stand self-proclaimed alpha males for very long: the guys who play a zero-sum dominance game; the guys perpetually surrounded by conflict; the guys who always need to be right: *my way or the highway*; the guys who always need to win at any cost; and the guys who lead with fear.

The first step to shedding this mask is, in a way, just embracing that fact. Just give yourself enough gut-check moments about the kind of behavior you see around you. It isn't enough to see it; you've got to see it and then have a reaction that's more critical than complimentary.

What's Available When You Drop This Mask (Alpha)

Remember Alpha Man, you are a gift, and there's so much to celebrate about you. The people who care about you the most have been waiting to see what's behind your mask. It's time to reveal the real you. These are some of the things that can flood back into your life when you drop this mask.

Win-win scenarios

Being the hero who lifts others up

The joy of being in service

Empowering others around you

Letting go of being in control

Freedom

Deeper sense of love

MEN:

Work for win-win scenarios in every possible circumstance. Use your energy to win and empower others to win. Instead of looking for things that separate us, look for things that unite us. Instead of looking for evidence that your way is the only way, try other people's ways. Listen, connect, and hear other people's ideas. **A true leader doesn't need to be right in order to feel worthy; he is able to see**

the best idea from anyone and bring it to light.

Anyone can win, but not everyone can create win-win. It would be a lie to say that it is going to be easy. I'm not asking you to change overnight. But I am asking you to start the process. And like so many other masks we've worked to remove with this book, it starts with asking and answering certain questions thoughtfully, openly, and honestly:

- ▶ What does losing mean to you?
- ▶ Why is your self-worth wrapped up in winning?
- ▶ What would be possible if everyone around you could win?
- ▶ What would be possible for you, your family, the world?

There's no growth in only doing things your way. Win-win is a whole other game, and it can give you a whole new lease on life. At the end of the day, the most important thing to remember is that we're all in this together.

WOMEN:

The next time you notice his Alpha Mask, don't back down. Your voice matters. Express to him that it's important for you to be heard. That you can both win. You don't need to agree to win—you can agree to disagree, and both of you can come out better for it. You can tell him in your own words that "I don't need to agree with you to love you." Winning simply means all involved parties are benefiting. Sometimes even in a loss there's a win. It's a perception. A viewpoint. Express how you feel when you're around him, in both a winning context and a losing context. Let him see how drastically different life is for you when he's focused on "being *the* man" instead of being *a gentle, caring* man. Society places a lot of value on being "the winner," but that phrase implies everyone else loses. With your support we can finally put a stop to those messages and create a win-win environment.

CONCLUSION

There are so many things I wish someone older and wiser had told me when I was a young man.

I was born in 1983, so obviously I wish that someone had told me to put my birthday money into Microsoft stock. Being from Ohio, I wish they'd have told me that I'd have to wait until I was 33 years old to see the Cavs win the NBA title and that I shouldn't hold my breath for the Cleveland Browns.

I wish someone—some man or woman I respected—had pulled me aside and said, "Lewis, masculinity is a bogus concept. You don't need to worry about being 'a man' or 'the man' or anything like that. Don't pretend to be anything or anyone except who you actually are. Do what you know is right and true; that's your only obligation as a man and as a human being."

Oh, how I wish someone had told me that, and how I wish I could have heard them. It would have saved me so much suffering. Suffering is a powerful word, but when I think back on my life, it is a word that defined my childhood.

And at the root of that suffering were my struggles with masculinity.

Until my late twenties, about all I was doing was suffering, especially during my teens and college years. The torment of my elementary school years—having trouble with reading, being big and awkward, enduring my fair share of bullying—was so profound, I could hardly stand to be alive. I just didn't think I deserved the privilege.

I wish I'd have known that I didn't need to prove to other people that I was a man. Even though I was born a male, I had yet to learn that the best thing I could do was love myself. I wish I'd have known to spend my time around people who supported me, not those who brought me down. Early on I think I surrounded myself with people who made me feel like I had to prove myself as a man, and I had to steal, cheat, lie, fight, and be aggressive in order to do that.

I wish I'd have known that I didn't have to suffer, constantly proving myself as a man. I wish I'd have known how to let go and forgive. Even now, knowing that intellectually doesn't make it any easier to live that way, to truly understand it in my soul and in my being. That's the struggle I have, and it's what drove me to explore this topic.

It's my belief that every book should begin from a pain point. A book that is intended to lecture or preach or theorize—what good is that to a reader? Does it really do anything for the author either? I don't think it does.

This book began from an acute pain point. I was at the top of my game and something felt off. I was alone, and though my life had many of the superficial markings of success, I wasn't happy. At an earlier stage in my life, I would have ignored those feelings. I would have tried on which-ever mask fit best to avoid the pain, and then put my best face forward. But I was able to do something different this time, and the journey I'd been on, up until that point, was what made it possible.

When I hear people talk about transformations and epiphanies, I am naturally suspicious. It doesn't work like that in my experience. I think it takes more than reading a book or attending a seminar to change a life. A drastic expe-rience is not enough either. There must be experience plus time, plus work . . . plus a real desire to change.

The exploration of my own masculinity began several years ago. I would discover a mask I wore and do the work to remove it. But then just as I thought I was clearer-headed, I would discover another mask. It was a journey of fits and spasms, peaks and valleys.

The crushing end of my sports career unearthed the Athlete Mask and the Aggressive Mask I'd lived behind for so many years, and it exposed the Invincible Mask and Joker Mask I wore to hide the pain. The overwhelming suc-cess of my business set the Material Mask in place, and the attention it garnered me added the Alpha Mask to my arse-nal as well. Going through breakups and coming to terms with the sexual abuse I had experienced as a child made me more aware of how easily I could slip back behind the Stoic Mask at the first sign of emotional pain while in a relation-ship (when I'd finally managed to make myself vulnerable). Meeting wonderful mentors and advisors—and their advice going right over my head—shined a light on the Know-It-All Mask that periodically sat between me and both personal and professional development.

It took one-on-one coaching, spiritual meditation retreats, deep conversations, trial and error, and time, but the hard work over time resulted in the making of the man I am today. By no means am I perfect, and I still have a lot of work to do, but I am more patient and forgiving, and a lot more loving. I don't hold on to the tension inside myself, and I don't hold on to the suffering like I used to. I'm not as resentful as I used to be. I think I've just taken the weight of proving myself off my own tired shoulders. It's not that I don't want to prove myself, it's that I no longer need to *prove it in order to be a man*. I have proven to myself that I am capable of creating what I truly want in life.

The biggest difference? I now feel I am able to be of service to others, to make an impact on others, and to make a difference to and for others. My thought process has changed from "How can I gain the most for myself?" to "How can I serve the most for other people?"

As I've said, this was a slow and gradual process, and I'm always a work in progress. I was partway down this path when I first watched Joe Ehrmann's TEDx Baltimore talk that I've told you so much about. I was further down it when I watched it for the third, fourth, and fifth times. I am further down it now as I watch it again, finishing this book. Each time I watch it, I get a better understanding of his words. I'll put them here for you to see them:

> *If you were on your deathbed today, knowing that you were going to die tomorrow, and you wanted to measure what kind of man you were and what kind of success you had in life, it'd come down to two things and two things only.*

The first is this: On that deathbed you recognize that all of life is about relationships. It's about the capacity to love and be loved. *What's it mean to be a man? It means you can look somebody in the eye and say "I love you" and receive that love back.*

You know what the questions you ask at the end of your life are? They're not about awards or achievements or applause or what you accumulated. They're all questions of relationships. What kind of husband was I? What kind of father? What kind of partner? What kind of son? What kind of friend? Who did I love and who did I allow to love me?

The second comes down to this: At the end of your life you want to be able to look back on your life and know that you made a difference. That you left some kind of mark, some kind of imprint, that you were here. *All of us want to leave some kind of legacy behind.*[1]

I wish I'd been told that when I was a young man. Maybe my parents and teachers and coaches did say it, but I was so stuck in my head that I wasn't able to hear anyone at the time.

I didn't go into much detail about my own father in this book, because I didn't want to make it all about me and my experience with masculinity. However, my beliefs on this topic first came from growing up around my parents. Although my dad has worn his versions of the Alpha, Know-It-All, and Aggressive masks, he has also shown a very loving, vulnerable side. Many times, I've seen him cry during movies that have moved him. I've seen him act calm, sweet, and tender toward my sisters and mom, and he has shown a sensitive side. He is affectionate, has always cared for our well-being, and would do anything to protect us. Seeing these contradictions in him, I felt equally conflicted in myself among all the pressures of peers, the locker room, and the media. I didn't know how to be my authentic self *and* be confident in who I was.

But I guess it's like that saying about planting a tree: The best time to plant one is 20 years ago, and the second best time is right now. Well, I'm not as young as I once was, but I am still young enough to hear Joe's advice and let it improve my life right now. The same is true for you.

| THE JOURNEY WE'VE GONE ON TOGETHER |

Over the last 200-plus pages (and in my case, hundreds of hours of conversations on the podcast), you and I have gone on a journey. We've explored everything we should have been told about masculinity when we were younger. We've explored what every young man should have been taught in school, at home, and on the playground.

Our aim was to counteract the myths, to reduce the need for masks. Masculinity is not about being the biggest, the fastest, the strongest, the one who sleeps with the most girls, and the one who has the most money. The one who has the most accomplishments is not the most masculine. In fact, it is often the men who covet these things most who are covering and compensating for the greatest insecurities. **Let us revere the one who loves others deeply, loves himself deeply, and has a dream that he is inspired to live with and by and through. He is a man.**

He does not stand unmoved or untouched in the face of truly moving experiences.

He does not judge the totality of his life or anyone else's life by the totals on the scoreboard as the clock ticks down to zero.

He does not use money as a proxy for emotional connection nor material possessions as the measure of his self-worth.

He does not define his manhood by the number of women he has conquered.

He does not always fight fire with fire; sometimes he doesn't need to fight at all.

He does not meet seriousness with silliness when it is seriousness that is required.

He does not take risks for risks' sake, because he does not hide from his frailty, his mortality, or his humanity.

He does not pretend to know everything about anything, nor is he afraid to admit when he knows nothing about something.

And perhaps most important of all, he does not walk around thinking he's *The Man*.

No, the masculine man goes through a journey, a process of self-discovery, and figures out what he needs to do to acquire the tools, knowledge, wisdom, grace, love, passion, and joy to pursue his destiny. His destiny is his dreams. Those may evolve over time, but in their pursuit, he is not breaking down anyone else or hurting anyone else. He is not at war with other people, conquering them. He is the one joining forces, searching for the win-win. He is the one who is lifting others up, inspiring others through his journey and his own process (in which he is finding ways to create value along the way). He is the hero of his own journey. And in so being, he is looking for every way to have the best relationships possible with his family, friends, his romantic partner, his colleagues, or his customers. He's finding ways to be the best possible version of himself.

Masculinity is about discovering yourself and owning what you find. It's about being kind to others, and pursuing your dreams with all the passion and energy you can muster. It's about doing something that is meaningful to you that brings value to others. That's how you build a legacy.

| ONWARD AND UPWARD |

I opened this book with the emotional inner battle I was fighting during my tour for *The School of Greatness*. It is not lost on me as I finish this book that soon enough I will be back on tour, back giving interviews, and back being the man in front of the camera.

Whereas the last time was dark and lonely, this time, I am fulfilled and excited.

Whatever the future has in store for me and my relationships, I am just so much more confident in who I am. I am detached from specific results. I am not concerned about things needing to be a certain way. I want to be open and honest and vulnerable to the people who have found something in these pages to connect with so that I can connect with them.

Of course that doesn't mean I won't get upset or frustrated or hurt by things that happen, but I am so much more grateful now—for life, for my family and friends, for opportunity—that I am confident the bad times will roll off my back like water into the dirt, from which good things will grow. I am excited just to show up in my life with joy, no matter what is going on. I'm excited to continue to give, and I am committed to being in service to others.

I think some men are afraid to give so much of themselves over to others, to things outside of themselves. They're worried that removing their masks will rob them of their edge, that it will soften them. I can tell you that this is a myth.

I think I'm always going to be a creator, bringing my ideas to life. The journey I have undergone has only made that clearer to me. If anything, it's sharpened my edge. Today, I am more excited than ever to create something of value in the world and be in service to people. I have learned that happiness and fulfillment are in the journey, not the destination, so I am not going to stop driving forward, or growing. And neither should any of you.

| NOW PAY IT FORWARD |

We talked a lot about masculinity in this book, but I have deliberately steered away from the tricky waters of biology and gender. I know nothing about those topics, although I do know about the basic propagation of our species.

Every man and woman is part of an unbroken biological chain. Even if you don't have children, you have relatives—however distant. We also have our spiritual relations—friends, colleagues, partners, students, teammates, even strangers with whom we share so much in common.

It's on us to help each other remove the masks of masculinity. It's on us to help others with questions that echo the opening of this chapter: What do I wish I'd known when I was a young man? What do I wish I'd been shown?

I've been clear that I underwent my journey through masculinity for somewhat selfish reasons. I wasn't motivated by the cause of gender equality. I am not an academic, studying this topic as an intellectual (although I've added academic research to this book to back up certain points). I began this journey simply as a way to address a pain point in my own life.

As I progressed, I found that the pain not only stopped—but that I got better at what I do. Like I said, this process has lifted a weight off my shoulders. I wrote this book in an excited sprint so that I could share what I was learning before I forgot any of it.

Now on the other side of my journey, my life is so much better that I am trying to pay it forward. I want to end this book on that note. **I hope that as you complete your journey—whether it's removing one mask or all nine—you will pay forward what you've learned too.** If you do, I'd love to hear your story about what has opened up for you in this process. Feel free to go to lewishowes.com and message me on my contact form to share what you have learned in your own unmasking.

If you have children—especially boys—please teach them what it really means to be a man.

If you have a brother, let him know you love him for who he is and support him.

If you are an aunt or an uncle, please teach your nieces and nephews to be themselves, not who society pressures them to be.

If you are a friend, create a safe space for men you know to admit when they don't know, when they feel pain, and when they are afraid.

If you have a platform or a fan base, please be authentic and real to the people who hang on your every word.

If you're an employer, recognize when your employees are struggling and help them.

If you're a coach, push your players to be *their* best, not *your* best or *society's* best.

If you're a partner, understand that your boyfriend or husband's greatest fear is the humiliation of letting you down, of not being enough.

It's great to remove your own masks. It's truly honorable and brave to help others do the same.

For me, I look at a man as a symbol of inspiration, someone who lives to be of service along his journey. He's someone who follows his purpose, who experiences fears but has the courage to face them and move forward anyway. He's someone who is loving to all people, creatures, and the world, himself included. He's someone who can take care of his basic needs and teach others how to live in abundance. He's someone who doesn't judge people but looks for ways to lift others up. And he's someone who leaves this place better than the way he found it.

That to me is a man.

ACKNOWLEDGMENTS

Thank you to my family, Diana, Ralph, Chris, Heidi, and Katherine, who taught me what unconditional love means and how to be the best man I can be. Thank you for accepting me exactly as I am and supporting me on this journey of healing and self-compassion. Your support, especially as I stepped into the scary waters of opening up about this topic, means the world to me. I'm so blessed to have you as family.

I want to thank Jen Esquer for her patience, love, and support with me on this journey and for understanding I'm not perfect and constantly learning how to be a better man.

To every mentor, teacher, and coach I've had who exemplified what it means to be a true man, thank you. You inspired me before I even knew what that meant.

To my agent, Stephen Hanselman, thanks for believing in me, especially with a topic that is vulnerable and challenging to discuss. You've supported me for years in bringing my visions into reality.

Thanks to Ryan Holiday and Nils Parker at Brass Check for writing this book with me and advising on the message and positioning along the way. You guys are the best. There is no way I could have done this without you.

To Marisa Vigilante, Danielle Curtis, Gail Gonzales, Jennifer Levesque and the entire family at Rodale, along with the amazing sales team including Jeffrey Capshew,

Allison Lazarus, Elena Guzman, and the rest of the powerful army, Yelena Nesbit, Aly Mostel, Angie Giammarino, and Amy King! Thanks for your tireless support in making this book the best it can be.

To my team that supported me for countless hours during the writing of this book, Matt Cesaratto, Sarah Livingstone, Brittany Fusco, Christine Baird, Aja Wiltshire, Tiffani Tyler, Lyonel Reneau, and Diana Howes—thank you! We are making a powerful impact together!

To everyone who inspired or contributed to *The Mask of Masculinity*, this wouldn't be possible without the incredible wisdom and truth that you have chosen to share with the world. I honor you and what you are standing for.

Rich Roll	Gabby Reece	Steve Cook
Ray Lewis	Rob Dyrdek	Tai Lopez
Steve Weatherford	Daymond John	Ryan Holiday
Travis Pastrana	Alanis Morissette	Neil Strauss
Tony Robbins	Maria Sharapova	Brendan Schaub
Chris Lee	Mike Rowe	JP Sears
Jennifer Siebel Newsom	Tim Ferriss	Tucker Max
	Shawn Johnson	Dan Harris
Joe Ehrmann	Eric Greitens	Donald Schultz
Larry King	Dr. Niobe Way	James Altucher
Taye Diggs	Dale Dye	Chris Voss
Russell Simmons	Christian Howes	Matthew Hussey
Arianna Huffington	Robbie Rogers	Brett McKay
Gary Vaynerchuk	Randy Couture	

To all my friends and supporters, thank you for listening, sharing, and inspiring me every step of the way! You make what I do possible. It means the world to me.

ENDNOTES

Introduction

1 A 2014 meta-analysis of sex differences in scholastic achievement published in the journal *Psychological Bulletin* found females outperformed males in teacher-assigned school marks throughout elementary, junior/middle, and high school, and at both undergraduate and graduate university level.

Voyer, Daniel, and Susan D. Voyer. "Gender Differences in Scholastic Achievement: A Meta-Analysis." *Psychological Bulletin* 140, no. 4 (2014): 1174–1204.

According to the National Center for Education Statistics, women earned more associate's, bachelor's, and master's degrees than men in the 2005–2006 academic year.

National Center for Education Statistics. "Historical Summary of Faculty, Students, Degrees, and Finances in Degree-Granting Institutions: Selected Years, 1869–70 through 2005–06." *Digest of Education Statistics* (2007): Table 178.

Women have outnumbered men on college campuses in the United States by a widening margin since the late 1970s.

National Center for Education Statistics. "Gender Differences in Participation and Completion of Undergraduate Education and How They Have Changed over Time." 2005, https://nces.ed.gov/das/epubs/pdf/2005169_es.pdf. Accessed January 1, 2017.

In a study by the Organisation for Economic Co-operation and Development (OECD) of 43 developed countries, 15-year-old girls were ahead of boys in literacy skills and were more confident than boys about getting high-income jobs. In the United States, girls are significantly ahead of boys in writing ability at all levels of primary and secondary education.

National Center for Education Statistics. "Percentage of Students Attaining Writing Achievement Levels, by Grade Level and Selected Student Characteristics: 2002." *Digest of Education Statistics* (2007): Table 119.

2 Moffitt, T.E., and A. Caspi. "Childhood Predictors Differentiate Life-Course Persistent and Adolescence-Limited Antisocial Pathways among Males and Females." *Development and Psychopathology* 13, no. 2 (2001): 355–75.

3 Males regardless of age engaged in more physical and verbal aggression than females, and males tend to engage in more unprovoked aggression at higher frequency than females.

Hyde, J.S. "Gender Differences in Personality and Social Behavior." *International Encyclopedia of the Social & Behavioral Sciences* (2001): 5989–994.

4 Men are more likely than women to use almost all types of illicit drugs, and illicit drug use is more likely to result in emergency department visits or overdose deaths for men than for women. In general, men have higher rates of alcohol use, including binge drinking. Fewer females than males use marijuana.

United States Department of Health and Human Services. Substance Abuse and Mental Health Services Administration. Center for Behavioral Health Statistics and Quality. National Survey on Drug Use and Health, 2013. ICPSR35509-v3. Ann Arbor, MI: Inter-university Consortium for Political and Social Research [distributor], http://doi.org/10.3886/ICPSR35509.v3.

Fattore, Liana, and Walter Fratta. "How Important Are Sex Differences in Cannabinoid Action?" *British Journal of Pharmacology* 160, no. 3 (2010): 544–48.

Male high school students who smoke marijuana report poor family relationships and problems at school more often than female students who smoke marijuana.

Butters, J.E. "Promoting Healthy Choices: The Importance of Differentiating between Ordinary and High Risk Cannabis Use among High-School Students." *Substance Use & Misuse* 40, no. 6 (2005): 845–55.

From 1999 to 2010, deaths from prescription pain reliever overdoses increased for men by 265 percent (CDC Vital Signs, 2013).

In 2010, about 27 men per day died from overdosing on prescription pain relievers, compared to 18 women per day (New CDC Vital Signs, 2013).

Mack, Karin A., Christopher M. Jones, and Leonard J. Paulozzi. "Vital Signs: Overdoses of Prescription Opioid Pain Relievers and Other Drugs among Women—United States, 1999–2010." *Morbidity and Mortality Weekly Report* 62, no. 26 (2013): 537–42.

5 Crime in the United States, 2015, table 37. https://ucr.fbi.gov/crime-in-the-u.s /2015/crime-in-the-u.s.-2015/tables/table-37.

6 Murphy, G.E. "Why Women Are Less Likely Than Men to Commit Suicide." *Comprehensive Psychiatry* 39 (1998): 165–75.

7 Möller-Leimkühler, A.M. "The Gender Gap in Suicide and Premature Death Or: Why Are Men So Vulnerable?" *European Archives of Psychiatry and Clinical Neuroscience* 253, no. 1 (2003): 1–8.

8 *The Mask You Live In.* Directed by Jennifer Siebel Newsom. The Representation Project, 2015, San Francisco, CA.

9 Vogel, David L., Patrick J. Heath, Y. Joel Wong (Ed), and Stephen R. Wester (Ed). "Men, Masculinities, and Help-Seeking Patterns." *APA Handbook of Men and Masculinities* (2016): 685–707.

10 Kagan, Celine. "Reading for Masculinity in the High School English Classroom." *Thymos* 6, no. 1/2 (Spring-Fall 2012): 213–19.

The Stoic Mask

1 Blosnich, John R., et al. "Disparities in Adverse Childhood Experiences Among Individuals with a History of Military Service." *JAMA Psychiatry* 71, no. 9 (2014): 1041–48.

2 McClintock, Elizabeth Aura. "Why Breakups Are Actually Tougher on Men." *Psychology Today,* December 19, 2014, www.psychologytoday.com/blog/it-s -man-s-and-woman-s-world/201412/why-breakups-are-actually-tougher-men (accessed March 20, 2017).

3 Knight, Phil. *Shoe Dog* (New York: Scribner, 2016): 137.

4 Brunstein, Joachim C., Gabriele Dangelmayer, and Oliver C. Schultheiss. "Personal Goals and Social Support in Close Relationships: Effects on Relationship Mood and Marital Satisfaction." *Journal of Personality and Social Psychology* 71, no. 5 (1996): 1006–19.

Seidman, Gwendolyn. "7 Ways You Can Help Your Partner Reach Their Goals." *Psychology Today,* January 5, 2015, *www.psychologytoday.com/blog/close -encounters/201501/7-ways-you-can-help-your-partner-reach-their-goals* (accessed March 20, 2017).

5 Schoenberg, Nara. "His Hidden Needs." *Chicago Tribune,* October 30, 2012.

6 McClintock. "Why Breakups Are Actually Tougher on Men."

7 Ruger, William, Sven E. Wilson, and Shawn L. Waddoups. "Warfare and Welfare: Military Service, Combat, and Marital Dissolution." *Armed Forces & Society* 29, no. 1 (2002): 85–107.

8 Sayers, Steven L., Victoria A. Farrow, Jennifer Ross, and David W. Oslin. "Family Problems among Recently Returned Military Veterans Referred for a Mental Health Evaluation." *Journal of Clinical Psychiatry* 70, no. 2 (2009): 163–70.

9 Freed, Betsy Bates and David Freed. "Aversion to Therapy: Why Won't Men Get Help?" *Pacific Standard,* June 25, 2012, https://psmag.com/aversion-to-therapy -why-won-t-men-get-help-7998d34f1d4e#.i5sjoy2jf (accessed March 20, 2017).

10 Hinds, Andy. "Messages of Shame Are Organized around Gender." *The Atlantic,* April 26, 2013, www.theatlantic.com/sexes/archive/2013/04/messages -of-shame-are-organized-around-gender/275322 (accessed March 20, 2017).

11 Gardner, Howard. *Frames of Mind* (New York: Basic Books, 1985): 254.

The Athlete Mask

1 *The Mask You Live In.* Directed by Jennifer Siebel Newsom. The Representation Project, 2015, San Francisco, CA.

2 Roderick, Martin. "Work, Self and the Transformation of Identity: A Sociological Study of the Careers of Professional Footballers." Department of Sociology University of Leicester, September 2003, 143.

3 Thele, Kyle. "Derrick Rose Has Missed More Games in 2 Years Than Tim Duncan Has in His Career." *Chicago Sun-Times,* June 24, 2016, www.chicago .suntimes.com/sports/derrick-rose-has-missed-more-games-in-2-years-than-tim -duncan-has-in-his-career (accessed March 20, 2017).

4 "Why Men Don't Talk About Their Emotions," YouTube video, 5:22, posted by Martin Phillips-Hing, November 22, 2013, www.youtube.com/watch?v=S5wJ8YDnoQA. Accessed January 1, 2017

5 Legato, Marianne J. *Why Men Die First: How to Lengthen Your Lifespan.* Reprint edition. (New York: St. Martin's Griffin, 2009).

6 Newman, Kyle. "There's No Such Thing as Winning an Argument." *Know No Limits* (blog), Move Beyond, August 22, 2013, www.movebeyond.net/know-no -limits/relationship/theres-no-such-thing-as-winning-an-argument (accessed March 20, 2017).

7 "The Scientific Basis for the Orcas Island Couples' Retreat." Gottman Private Couples' Retreats, www.gottmancouplesretreats.com/about/relationships -dysfunctional-divorce-predictors.aspx (accessed March 20, 2017).

The Sexual Mask

1 Neil Strauss. "Inside an 'Anything Goes' Sex Club," blog of Tim Ferriss, http:// tim.blog/2015/10/13/polyamory/#more-22048. Accesed January 1, 2017.

2 Blazina, Chris, Rachel Eddins, Andrea Burridge, and Anna Settle. "The Relationship between Masculinity Ideology, Loneliness, and Separation-Individuation Difficulties." *The Journal of Men's Studies* 15, no. 1 (2007): 101–9.

The Aggressive Mask

1 Pollack, William. "Gender Issues: Modern Models of Young Male Resilient Mental Health." *Young Adult Mental Health,* edited by Jon E. Grant and Marc N. Potenza (Oxford University Press, 2009): 96–109.

2 Samaran, Nora. "The Opposite of Rape Culture Is Nurturance Culture." NoraSamaran.com. February 11, 2016.

3 Pollack. "Gender Issues: Modern Models of Young Male Mental Health."

4 C.A. Robarcheck, "Ghosts and Witches: The Psychocultural Dynamics of Semoi Peacefulness," in *The Anthropology of Peace and Nonviolence,* edited by L.E. Sponsel and T. Gregor (London: Lynne Rienner, 1994): 69–108.

5 Ibid.

6 Weeks, Linton. "Why Are Most Rampage Shooters Men?" NPR, *The Photojournalist,* September 24, 2013. www.npr.org/sections/thephotojournalist /2013/09/24/225689775/why-are-most-rampage-shooters-men.

7 Hamblin, James. "Toxic Masculinity and Murder." *The Atlantic,* June 16, 2016. Web.

The Joker Mask

1 Barrie, Zara. "There's Pain in Laughter." *EliteDaily,* http://elitedaily.com/life /culture/why-funniest-people-saddest/1057843, June 9, 2015. Accessed January 1, 2017.

2 McRady, Rachel. "Minnie Driver Remembers Robin Williams in Touching *Good Will Hunting* Story." *Us Weekly,* October 16, 2014, www.usmagazine.com /celebrity-news/news/minnie-driver-touching-robin-williams-good-will-hunting -story-20141610 (accessed March 20, 2017).

3 Barrie. "There's Pain in Laughter."

4 Sifferlin, Alexandra. "The Psychology of the Sad Clown." *Time,* August 13, 2014, www.time.com/3104938/depression-comedy-connection (accessed March 20, 2017).

5 Fisher, Seymour, and Rhoda L. Fisher. *Pretend the World Is Funny and Forever: A Psychological Analysis of Comedians, Clowns, and Actors* (Mahwah, NJ: L. Erlbaum Associates, 1981).

6 Vankin, Deborah. "Laugh Factory to Add Therapy to Stand-Up Comics' Routine." *Los Angeles Times,* February 9, 2011. Accessed January 1, 2017.

7 McGraw, Peter, and Joel Warner. "The Humor Code: Entry 9." *Slate,* April 2, 2014, http://www.slate.com/authors.joel_warner.html.

8 Lyubansky, Mikhail. "Robin Williams and the Mask of Humor." *Psychology Today*, August 11, 2014, www.psychologytoday.com/blog/between-the-lines/201408/robin-williams-and-the-mask-humor (accessed March 20, 2017).

9 Kring, Ann, and Albert Gordon. "Sex differences in emotion: expression, experience, and physiology," *Journal of Personality and Social Psychology*. 1998 Mar; 754(3):686-703. https://www.ncbi.nlm.nih.gov/pubmed/9523412. Accessed August 7, 2017.

10 Hyde, Eric. "Freud on Humor, and some Personal Insights." Eric Hyde's Blog, December 14, 2013, https://ehyde.wordpress.com/2013/12/14/freud-on-humor-and-some-personal-insights. Accessed January 1, 2017.

11 *The Mask You Live In.* Dir. John Behrens and Jennifer Siebel Newsom. Feat. Dr. Michael Kimmel, Dr. Caroline Heldman, Joe Ehrmann, Dr. Lise Eliot, and Dr. Michael Thompson. The Representation Project, 2015. Film.

The Invincible Mask

1 "Why Travis Pastrana Is the Man." LAT34, August 28, 2006. www.lat34.com/dew_tour/why_travis_pastrana_is

2 Gallagher, Brian. "Kevin Feige Talks Ant-Man and Marvel's Relationships with Directors." MovieWeb.com, April 2016. http://movieweb.com/kevin-feige-talks-ant-man-and-marvels-relationships-with-directors/

3 Mooney, Michael. "Terrell Owens's Darkest Days." *Grantland*, June 24, 2012, http://grantland.com/features/the-full-story-terrell-owens-time-allen-wranglers-indoor-football-league. Accessed January 1, 2017.

4 Meth, Richard L., and Robert S. Pasick. *Men in Therapy: The Challenge of Change* (New York: The Guilford Press, 1991): 14.

The Know-It-All Mask

1 Rosin, Hanna, and Alix Spiegel. *Invisibilia.* NPR. June 17, 2016. http://www.npr.org/programs/invisibilia/481887848/the-new-norm.

2 Ibid.

3 Lanpher, Katherine. "Little Bit of Sugar." *Marie Claire*, July 6, 2012, http://www.marieclaire.com/culture/a7221/cheryl-strayed-interview. Accessed January 1, 2017.

4 Altucher, James. "What Does It Feel Like to Lose a Lot of Money Quickly?" *Forbes*, April 10, 2013, https://www.forbes.com/sites/quora/2013/04/10/what-does-it-feel-like-to-lose-a-lot-of-money-quickly/#858763749868. Accessed January 1, 2017.

5 Ibid.

6 Bates, Laura. "Mansplaining: How Not to Talk to Female NASA Astronauts." *The Guardian,* September 13, 2016.

The Alpha Mask

1 Harris, Glenn. "2 Huge Insecurities All 'Alpha Males' Hide (as Written by One)." *Your Tango* blog, September 1, 2015, http://www.yourtango.com/experts /glenn-harris/2-huge-insecurities-alpha-men-hide-as-written-by-one.

2 Ibid.

3 Ibid.

4 Taylor, Christopher. "Bros Like Me: Adherence to Male Role Norms in Fraternity Men." Electronic Thesis or Dissertation, Miami University, 2015, https://etd .ohiolink.edu/pg_10?0::NO:10:P10_ETD_SUBID:109461.

5 Ibid.

Conclusion

1 Ehrmann, Joe. "Be a Man." TEDx Talk, posted online February 20, 2013, https:// www.youtube.com/watch?v=jVI1Xutc_Ws. Accessed January 1, 2017.

INDEX

A

Adolescence
  anger in, 112–14
  Sexual Mask adopted in, 87–88
  struggles with masculinity in,
    87–90
Aggression
  author's struggle with, 114–17
  as backwards nurturance, 116, 122
  in cage fighting, 109–11
  defining character through, 120
  domestic violence, 126–27
  in football, 111, 115
  in human history, 111–12
  learning to channel, 121, 128–29
  in male development, 112,
    113–14
  mass shootings, 125–26
  peaceful cultures and, 124, 125
  in sexuality, 94–95
  testosterone no excuse for,
    124–25
  unchanneled, 121–22
  usefulness of, 117
  in wresting, 120–21
Aggressive Mask, 109–30
  anger holding in place, 112–13, 118
  Athlete Mask with, 121
  author's, 114–16
  benefits of removing, 129
  childhood issues in, 110, 111, 117–
    18, 122, 128
  cultural influences on, 113–14
  emotional education lacking with,
    123–24
  emotions behind, 123
  Joker Mask and, 149
  learning to channel aggression,
    121, 128–29
  need to understand, 114
  overview, 9
  Randy Couture example, 117–21
  Ray Lewis example, 111,
    119–20, 127–28
  steps for removing, 130
  women and, 126–27, 130

Alpha Mask, 195–212
  author's, 202, 204
  behavior change with, 204
  body image concerns with, 200
  challenges of removing, 202–3
  confused understanding of, 199
  control and respect demanded
    with, 196–97
  evolved version of, 206–9
  exhaustion with, 207
  in fraternity culture, 203–4
  hostage negotiation and,
    196–98
  life after removing, 210
  lopsided development with,
    205–6
  overview, 10
  situations triggering, 195
  social pressure to maintain, 201–
    2, 203, 204
  in sports, 199, 201
  unattractiveness of, 206, 209–10
  validation with, 205
  weakness of, 197, 198, 199–200
  win-win scenarios for removing,
    210–11
  women and, 204–5, 206, 211–12
Altucher, James, 183–86
Anger. *See also* Aggression
  in adolescence, 112–14
  Aggressive Mask held in place by,
    112–13, 118
  author's, 115, 116, 117
  benefits of giving up, 127
  usefulness of, 117
  video games dominated by, 113
Arenas, Gilbert, 44
Armor, masks as, 7
Athlete Mask, 41–60
  Aggressive Mask with, 121
  author's, 42, 46, 53
  benefits of, 43
  competitiveness with, 51–52, 53
  cutting against the grain of,
    45–46
  dark side of, 44
  gym overexertion and, 49–50

233

having it ripped off, 54–57
hiding inside, 46
inevitable athletic decline and, 47,
51
Joe Ehrmann example, 41–43, 44,
46
life after removing, 58–59
obsession with sports and, 48–49
overview, 8–9
playing through pain and,
47–48
self-care not respected with, 48
self-worth overlooked by, 58
steps for removing, 59–60
Steve Cook example, 43, 46–47,
50
Steve Weatherford example,
54–57
virtues learned by athletes, 50–51
women and, 51–52, 53, 60

B

Beliefs, faulty assumptions of,
35–36
Biology, 96, 221
Bol, Manute, 45
Brown, Jason, 44–45

C

Cage fighting, 109–11
Cona, Andy, 110–11
Cook, Steve, 43, 46–47, 50
Couture, Randy, 117–21
Crittenton, Javaris, 44
Cromartie, Antonio, 44
Crying, 22, 34
Cultural influences
on aggression, 113–14, 124, 125
countering traditional
masculinity, 139
pressures to be alpha, 201–2, 203,
204
reinforcing masks, 165
on sexuality, 96–97, 101–2

D

Death. *See also* Invincible Mask
deathbed reflections, 216–17
early due to masculine notions, 2,
148–49
Divorce, predictors of, 51
Domestic violence, 126–27

Driver, Minnie, 134
Dye, Dale, 29–32
actors trained by, 18–19, 31–32
advice to younger self by, 30–31
appearance of, 19
emotions suppressed by, 23–24,
31–32
on facing life, 23
military achievements of, 18
reasons for interviewing, 19–20
relationships and, 27, 29
on sharing feelings, 24
Teehan as inspiration to,
20–21

E

Ehrmann, Joe
on the Athlete Mask as a lie, 43,
44, 46
athletic prowess of, 41–42
on deathbed reflections, 216–17
on the end of the athletic career,
47
Emotions. *See also* Anger; Fear
avoided with humor, 148–50
expressed by real men, 34
gender and expression of,
145–46
importance of understanding, 36
Invincible Mask hiding, 158
journaling about, 35, 39
poverty and, 68
sexual intimacy and, 99–102, 103,
105
sharing feelings, 24, 35–37, 39
Stoic Mask and suppression of, 21,
22, 23–24, 31–33, 34–35

F

Fear
behind the Aggressive Mask, 123
courage to admit, 143–44
faulty assumptions built on, 35
Invincible Mask hiding, 158
of labeling, Sexual Mask and,
93–94
men taught to ignore, 155
not letting other men see yours,
21
refusal to admit, 164
of vulnerability, 8, 13, 60, 104, 143,
178

Feelings. *See* Emotions
Fox, Rick and Roger, 180–81
Fraternity culture, 203–4
Freedom, illusion of, 84–85, 91

G

Gratitude, 80, 81–82

H

Happiness
    giving vs. receiving and, 76–78
    inconspicuous consumption and,
        75
    money and, 67–68, 74
    after removing Material Mask, 79
Harrington, Ray, 138–40
Harris, Dan, 166–68
Heroes
    Dye as paradigm of, 18–21, 23–24,
        27, 29–32
    emotions suppressed by, 21, 22,
        23–24, 31–33
    fantasies about, 17–18
Howes, Christian, 21–23
Howes, Louis
    Alpha Mask of, 202
    Athlete Mask of, 42, 46, 53
    basketball court fight of, 198–99
    brother's imprisonment and,
        21–23
    changes with this book, 220–21
    competitive streak in, 53
    disclaimer by, 14
    dishonesty as a youth, 158–63
    experience of being picked last,
        5–7
    focus on others by, 135–36
    hero dreams of, 18
    on his father's character, 217–18
    knowledge he wishes he'd had,
        213–14, 217
    marital life of, 104
    Material Mask of, 66, 68–69,
        71–72
    near-rape experience of, 98–99
    raped as young child, 36–37,
        97–98
    reasons for interviewing Dye,
        19–20
    Stoic Mask of, 21–23, 32–33
    struggles with aggression by,
        114–17

    struggles with masculinity by,
        213–14
    struggles with sexuality by,
        88–89, 91–92, 93, 97, 98–99
    work on masks by, 215–16
Humor. *See also* Joker Mask
    defensive, 135, 141, 149
    drug-like effects of, 132
    emotions avoided by, 148–50
    mean, 146–48
    need for, 150
    pain deflected by, 135, 136, 143–45
    positive vs. detrimental, 151
    self-defeating, 140
    as self-medication, 140

I

Inesta, Andres, 45–46
Invincible Mask, 153–74
    adrenaline addiction with, 172
    assessing risks as antidote to,
        169–70
    awareness of needs despite,
        168
    broader application of, 165
    cultural reinforcement of, 165
    Dan Harris example, 166–68
    dishonesty hidden by, 158–63
    downsides of, 155–56, 158
    emotions hidden by, 158
    invincibility not the truth,
        156–58, 163
    life after removing, 157, 172–73
    memento mori practice and, 170–
        71
    overview, 10
    questions for countering,
        173–74
    remembering our humanity as
        antidote to, 170–72
    self-neglect with, 164–65
    stories given power by, 166–68,
        170
    Travis Patrana example,
        153–57
    women and, 174
    in workaholism, 167

J

Joker Mask, 131–52. *See also* Humor
    acceptance won by, 138
    Aggressive Mask and, 149

author's, 137
courage needed for removing, 143–44
distancing with, 142, 143, 148–49
focus on others and, 135–36
insecurities beneath, 137, 141
Laugh Factory therapy program, 141–42
life after removing, 151–52
mean humor with, 146–48
need to look beneath, 150–51
overview, 9–10
pain deflected by, 135, 136, 143–45
Ray Harrington example, 138–40
Robin Williams example, 131–35, 140, 144
sadness beneath, 136, 140, 145
steps for removing, 152
Tucker Max example, 142–44
women and, 152
in young boys, 145–47
Journaling, 35, 39
Journey of masculinity, 218–20

K

Knight, Phil, 25–26
Know-It-All Mask, 175–94
authentic humility vs., 186–87, 192
author's experience with, 181–82
challenges of removing, 192
defined, 177
false picture of, 178
foolishness due to, 187
insecurities beneath, 191
life after removing, 193–94
listening to get beyond, 176–77, 191, 192–93, 194
mansplaining with, 190–91
mistaken "experts" with, 188
not admitting you don't know, 181
overcompensation with, 177–78
overview, 10
persuasion hampered by, 183
prevalence of, 177
professional lives affected by,
179–81
Ursa oil rig and, 179–81
the wisdom of not knowing vs., 182–83
women and, 194

L

Laugh Factory therapy, 141–42
Lewis, Ray, 111, 119–20, 127–28
Listening
importance of skill in, 176–77
Know-It-All Mask removed by, 192–93, 194
learning from all you meet, 191
Lopez, Tai
age hidden by, 63–64
avid reading by, 63
conspicuous wealth of, 61–62, 65–66, 70
on the dangers of money, 66
entrepreneurship of, 65
ideas devalued by, 70–71
on inconspicuous consumption, 75
poverty in early life of, 64–65
PR blitz by, 62–63
Robbins compared to, 78
Salatin's influence on, 64
self-worth seen materially by, 72–73
split opinions about, 69–70
Love
as part of prosperity, 57
prevented by Stoic Mask, 27
by real men, 217, 219
for yourself, 106–7, 122

M

Mansplaining, 190–91
Masculinity, traditional
adolescent struggle with, 87–90
athletic ability associated with, 43
cultural counters to, 139
current reality of, 31–32
deconstructing the myth of, 4–5, 218–20
emotional suppression with, 34–35
growth prevented by notions of, 36

ills due to notions of, 1–2, 13
mass shootings and, 126
notions of, 1, 4
relationships and, 27–29
"solutions" proposed for, 2–3
Masks, in general. *See also specific masks*
as armor, 7
benefits of removing, 11, 12, 216
challenges of removing, 11–12
cultural reinforcement of, 165
helping each other remove, 222–23
problems disguised by, 163–64
real self lost due to, 10–11
as traps, 3
types of masks, 8–10
Mass shootings, 125–26
Material Mask, 61–82. *See also Money*
author's, 66, 68–69, 71–72
the dangers of money, 66
evolution and drive toward, 66
fame desired with, 73
gratitude for countering, 80, 81–82
happiness and money, 67–68
ideas devalued by, 70–71
life after removing, 78, 79, 80
overview, 9
poverty as driver for, 64–65, 67, 68–69
provider role and, 66–67
self-worth and, 68–69, 80
Tai Lopez example, 61–66, 69–73, 75, 78
value vs. success and, 74–75
women and, 82
Max, Tucker, 99–101, 103, 142–44
Memento mori, 170–71
Men
early death of, 2, 148–49
emotions and gender, 145–46
purpose of this book for, 3
social problems of, 1–2
suicide rates and gender, 2, 148–49
Military service, 18–19, 23
Money. *See also* Material Mask
giving vs. receiving, 76–78
happiness and, 67–68, 74
inconspicuous consumption with, 75

poverty, 64–65, 67, 68–69
relationships not bought with, 75–76
self-worth and, 68–69
Morissette, Alanis, 73, 74–75, 208

N
Negotiation with alphas, 196–98

P
Pain
deflected by humor, 135, 136, 143–45
playing sports through, 47–48
refusal to admit, 164
Pastrana, Travis
awareness of mortality by, 154, 156–57
death-defying feats of, 153–54
injuries sustained by, 154
Invincible Mask removed by, 157
Paying it forward, 222–23
Pornography, 94–95
Poverty, 64–65, 67, 68–69. *See also* Material Mask
Prosperity, defined, 57

R
Relationships. *See also* Sexual Mask
as key to success, 12, 27–28
not for purchase, 75–76
traditional masculinity and, 27–29
Robbins, Tony, 76–79
Rogers, Robbie, 26–27
Roner, Erik, 156
Rose, Derrick, 48
Rowe, Mike, 175–76, 187–90

S
Schaub, Brendan, 92
Schultz, Donald, 169–70
Self-worth
fame not a solution for, 73
loving yourself, 106–7
Material Mask and, 68–69, 80
material view of, 72–73
self-deprecating humor and, 140
sexual conquest and, 85, 86–88, 89–90
sources of, 58
Semoi of Malaysia, 124, 125

Sexual abuse
    author's experiences with, 36–37,
        97–99
    military service correlated to, 23
Sexual Mask, 83–107
    adoption in adolescence, 87–88
    aggression with, 94–95
    author's struggle with, 88–89,
        91–92, 93, 97, 98–99
    biology as excuse for, 96
    cultural myths and, 96–97, 101–2
    disappointing nature of, 86–87, 93
    emotional connection and,
        99–102, 103, 105
    ethical issues with, 87, 93
    exhaustion with, 87, 91, 92
    fear of labeling and, 93–94
    illusion of freedom with, 84–85,
        91
    life after removing, 102–4, 105–6
    marital sex and, 102, 103–4
    Neil Strauss example, 83–86,
        89–91, 93, 95, 97, 102
    nightmare vs. dream with, 83–85,
        98
    overview, 9
    self-worth and, 85, 86–88,
        89–90
    steps for removing, 106–7
    Tucker Max example, 99–101, 103
    women and, 107
Sports. See Athlete Mask
Stoic Mask, 17–40
    author's, 21–23, 32–33
    benefits of removing, 26–27, 37
    Dale Dye example, 18–21, 23–24,
        27, 29–32
    disease created by, 38
    emotional suppression with, 21,
        22, 23–24, 31–33, 34–35
    getting help with, 39–40
    heroes demonstrating, 17–22
    journey to remove, 35
    life after removing, 38
    love prevented by, 27
    overview, 8
    Phil Knight example, 25–26
    real you hidden by, 26
    relationships and, 27–28
    Robbie Rogers example, 26–27
    sharing feelings despite, 24, 39
    steps for removing, 38–40
    women and, 25–26, 40

Strauss, Neil
    adolescent anxieties of, 89–90
    childhood issues of, 95
    dream turned into nightmare for,
        84–85
    hitting bottom by, 90–91, 93
    on marital sex, 102
    as master pickup artist, 83–84,
        85–86
    seeing himself as the problem, 97
Suicide rates and gender, 2,
        148–49

T
Teehan, "Wild Bill," 20–21
Testosterone, 124–25

U
Ursa oil rig, 179–81

V
Video games, anger dominating, 113
Violence. See Aggression
Voss, Chris, 196–98, 199, 209
Vulnerability. See also Invincible
        Mask
    appropriate, 200–201
    fear of, 8, 13, 60, 104, 143, 178
    truth and courage with, 13

W
Wealth. See Material Mask; Money
Weatherford, Steve, 54–57
Williams, Robin, 131–35, 140, 144
Women. See also Sexual Mask
    Aggressive Mask and, 126–27, 130
    Alpha Mask and, 204–5, 206,
        211–12
    Athlete Mask and, 51–52, 53, 60
    benefits of this book for, 14–15
    domestic violence against,
        126–27
    as emotionally educated, 123
    Invincible Mask and, 174
    Joker Mask and, 152
    Know-It-All Mask and, 194
    Material Mask and, 82
    objectification of, 87
    purpose of this book for, 3–4
    Sexual Mask and, 107
    Stoic Mask and, 25–26, 40
Workaholism, 167

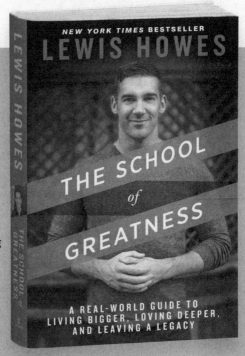